Alverti

may God continue to bless you in everything

Much Love,
Keila B.

Recrowning God's Daughters

An Anthology

TENITA C. JOHNSON

Published by So It Is Written, LLC
Detroit, MI
SoItIsWritten.net

Recrowning God's Daughters: An Anthology
Copyright © 2022 by Tenita C. Johnson

All rights reserved. No part of this book may be reproduced or transmitted in any form or by any means, electronic or mechanical, including photocopying, recording, or by an information storage and retrieval system—except by a reviewer who may quote brief passages in a review to be printed in a magazine or newspaper—without permission in writing from the official publisher.

Edited by: So It Is Written – www.SoItIsWritten.net

Formatting: Ya Ya Ya Creative – www.YaYaYaCreative.com

ISBN: 979-8-9850206-9-4

LCCN: 2022907066

PRINTED AND BOUND IN THE UNITED STATES OF AMERICA

Table of Contents

Dr. Jekyll And Mr. Hyde – *Cierra Warren* 1
    Recrowning & Reflection 19
    About The Author 21

Pieces of A Crown – *Dr. Teresa B. Moore* 23
    Recrowning & Reflection 41
    About The Author 43

Weathering The Storms of Life While
in Full Pursuit of My Purpose – *Dr. Cherie Cofield* 47
    Recrowning & Reflection 63
    About The Author 65

The Prodigal Daughter – *Tenita C. Johnson* 67
    Recrowning & Reflection 81
    About The Author 83

Unveiled – *Dr. Kathleen Abate* 87
    Recrowning & Reflection 109
    About The Author 111

Tainted Lens – *LaShana R. Anderson* 113
    Recrowning & Reflection 131
    About The Author 133

The False Crown – *Ronisse P. White* 135
   Recrowning & Reflection 149
   About The Author 151

Crowned Identity – *Nicho Charisse* 153
   Recrowning & Reflection 167
   About The Author 169

The Lost & Crown – *Siobhan R. Flynn* 171
   Recrowning & Reflection 183
   About The Author 185

The Art of Forgiveness – *Keila D. Brintley* 187
   Recrowning & Reflection 201
   About The Author 203

The Crooked Crown – *Claira Smith* 205
   Recrowning & Reflection 217
   About The Author 219

The Bent & Broken Crown – *Deanna M. Ferguson* 221
   Recrowning & Reflection 237
   About The Author 239

About So It Is Written 241

Dr. Jekyll and Mr. Hyde

Cierra Warren

"My cousin wants to talk to you," I saw as I read the text message from my home girl Shay.

I replied, "About a cake?"

"No, girl! He thinks you're cute. He asked for your number."

"Your cousin who?"

She sent me a picture right after that text. He wasn't skinny, but he wasn't too big either. He was taller than me, brown-skinned and had nice teeth. He dressed casually. I didn't care for the flashy earring in his ear or the Chrysler 300 he was posing in front of, but hopefully that meant he had his own car.

"Not bad," I replied. "Does he have kids?"

"No."

"Does he have his own place?"

She replied, "Yes."

"Does he work?"

"Yes."

"You can give him my number."

A few moments later, I received a text from a random number. It was Shay's cousin. I found out his name was Allen. I laughed because he didn't look like an Allen. He asked if he could call me, and I agreed. Before I knew it, I was roaming around outside, playing twenty-one questions with this random guy who seemed to want to get to know me.

We talked about favorite drinks, hobbies and everything surface level. I found out he was an active member of his church where he was the head of a mime group. He told me how his group traveled all over and performed at different places in the city. I was impressed to know that he was active in church because I was, too. Church is a big part of my foundation.

About a month ago, I had moved from Saginaw back home to Pontiac, Michigan after graduating college a few months prior. I was offered a management job not far from my parents' home and I was excited. I had just made a vow to refocus on God and the things He would have me do in this new season. I planned to work, sign up for evening classes, establish an exercise regimen, and, most importantly, become celibate. I wasn't going to rush into dating. I was never one to be promiscuous; however, given my past relationships, I was not ready to put effort into dating. I decided to move back home with my parents to save money for a condominium.

There I was, three weeks into this new "vow" and I'd met someone. I figured it was God. This time, I wasn't looking for anything. It came to me. I had also just refocused on my goals. You know what *they* say: "God will send you what you need when you are not looking for it." I did not know if anything would come of talking to Allen because I literally had just met him. However, he sounded like a pretty good guy.

Days and weeks went by as Allen and I communicated daily. Some days, we only sent a few texts. Other days, we spent hours on the phone. After talking to him quite often, I became interested in taking things further. He was charming and attentive. He seemed responsible. I paid attention to the many times he got off the phone with me to go to work or to pay bills. I most definitely was attracted to that! I was twenty-four and he was twenty-five. This was the first time since high school that I was interested in talking to someone close to my age. I was always very mature, so I naturally attracted older men. Honestly, I didn't think I would find a man my age who was on my level. Not to toot my own horn, but I had just graduated college, had a management job, and was a four-year business owner. I was also driving one of my favorite cars. I was doing alright for a twenty-four-year-old.

I hadn't seen Shay since I'd moved back to Pontiac. So, I decided to meet up with her one Saturday after a pop-up shop dessert sale. I booked a hotel room so I could sleep over and already be in town for church the next day. Although I had moved back to my hometown, my church was in Saginaw. I continued to drive for service every Sunday and Tuesday for Bible study. Shay and I met up and she invited her cousin Allen to dinner. We chatted for a bit and hugged before he left. He suggested that we get together soon—just the two of us. I thought that would be a good idea since we were trying to get to know each other.

Allen and I continued to talk often, and he mentioned that he wanted to come support me at my upcoming business event. Him and Shay rented a hotel room in Auburn Hills so they would be close by. Shay and Allen joined me for dinner with all my friends. The next day, they showed up at my parents' house to help load up the vehicles for my event. This was the first time Allen met my mom.

When she saw him, she said, "Okay! So, you're the Allen I've been hearing about. Very nice and handsome!"

I was shocked to see my mom so engaging because she did not like any of my male friends. Allen asked what he could do to help, and he literally did everything I needed him to do. He loaded and unloaded the cars. He set up and broke down tables. He even helped clean. I was impressed, and so were my parents. Before my event started, I needed to go home to get dressed. Allen asked to ride with me. In the car, we shared small talk. He opened the door of the car for me, even though I was driving. He carried my clothes into the house, and he carried a load of things to the car. This was weird. I'd never had a man be so kind, but I enjoyed it all.

When the weekend was over, I really liked Allen. My family liked him, too. My cousins and aunts asked if he had brothers jokingly. He was handsome and helpful. He seemed to be the perfect gentleman.

Since Allen had met a lot of my family, he wanted me to meet his family. He asked me to come to church with him the following week. I was nervous, but I wanted to make a good impression. So, I put on my Sunday's best and went to church with him. Allen met me in Saginaw because his church was in Bay City, and he wanted to ride together. He picked me up from a shopping center and we headed to church. I was worried about us being late, but he assured me that service wouldn't start on time. During church, he was up and down a lot. I was struggling to stay awake because this church was much slower paced than what I was used to. After church, I met many people. His mom wasn't at church that day, so we went by her house so I could meet her. She came outside and we talked briefly. She told me I was beautiful and told me that Allen would treat me well.

Afterward, Allen and I went to a restaurant in Midland, Michigan. I'd never heard of this restaurant, but it was far out, which allowed us a lot of time to talk during the car ride. We had a nice dinner and, on the way back to my car, he asked me about what I was looking for in a relationship. I shared a little bit of information about my past relationships, and I told him I wanted to date someone with purpose. I explained that my end goal was marriage.

He said, "Oh! So, you want to get married?"

I said, "Yes! I already have my ring picked out!"

He wanted to see the ring. He suggested that we go to the mall to look at rings, but the mall was closed. He was joking, but his interest in being married attracted me even more to him. We talked for a while longer and he handed me a big box. Inside was a cute pink purse with a necklace and bracelet to match. Sweetest Day had passed a week or so ago. However, we weren't official, so I didn't expect a gift. That made me feel special. We hugged before I got into my car to go home. But, this time, the hug felt different. It was a hug that you share with someone you *like*. The whole ride home, I was smiling and excited. It seemed like the seventy-five-minute drive was over in moments.

My mom saw me walk into the house with the box and she asked to see what was in it. I smiled and showed her, then I went to show my dad. I was giddy. Allen was earning more brownie points with my parents by the minute.

Even though we hadn't become a couple yet, we spent a lot of time together. Thanksgiving was fast approaching, and his mom asked me to make the cake for their family dinner. Their family was so big that they rented a hall to host Thanksgiving dinner. I spent Thanksgiving with his family, and he spent Christmas with mine. At Thanksgiving, I was introduced as his *friend*. By Christmas, I was his *girlfriend*.

At the top of the next year, Allen and I went on a couple's trip to Chicago. That was the first time we spent a whole night together. Still, he was the perfect gentleman. He didn't try to pressure me into sleeping with him. We didn't even kiss. We didn't want to rush things once we got serious. Sex was not on the table. We just wanted to get to know each other.

We talked every day. We saw each other on the weekends. We spent birthdays together, and we seemed like we were growing together as a couple. At family gatherings, he told people that I was going to be his wife. Hearing him say that gave me butterflies.

After almost a year of dating, I moved in with him. His house was not my favorite. In fact, I could not believe I agreed to live there. I guess it was love that made me endure the house. Or it may have been the fact that he promised to fix it up or move us to something better eventually. Throughout my time living with Allen, I found out many hard truths. Allen did not own his house, like he told me he did. His mom owned it. He barely made his monthly payments on the house. The car that he was posing in front of was in his mom's name, too. He wasn't paying the car note or insurance. To top it all off, Allen was not that great of an employee. He called into work often just because he wanted to. He lost several jobs while we were together, including the one I got him in my hometown. Allen was good with his words, and he said things to make me believe he wanted to do better and be better.

It was hard sharing a living space with Allen because he was selfish. He constantly stayed out all night and came home drunk. Sometimes, he didn't come home until after 5 a.m. Many times, he ignored my calls while he was out. When he would finally come home, I had an attitude and didn't want to talk to him. A few times, we ended up in heated arguments. One time, we tore up the house while fighting. One night, he even left me at the bakery all night with no ride home. I had to walk home at midnight. I was for sure done with him after that.

The next day, I packed my bags and called my dad to get me. Allen rushed out the house to try to explain what happened. Somehow, we ended up driving an hour and a half to have a talk with my parents. Allen had a terrible habit of calling my parents whenever we had a disagreement. My parents asked us if we really wanted to be together because our relationship did not seem healthy. That day, I ended up going back to Bay City with Allen. My parents had to give us gas money because neither of us had any.

I found myself constantly giving to Allen. Whether it was for gas, a phone bill that was constantly disconnected, or money for bills that were so far behind, it was hard to catch up. A part of me felt like some of the things we were going through would simply make us stronger as a couple. He was good at smoothing things over or talking his way out of bad situations.

Before I knew it, we were engaged. We had talked about getting married and started moving in that direction, although he had not purchased a ring or officially proposed to me. Allen asked my parents' permission to marry me and, surprisingly, they approved. Both of our families seemed extremely excited. We planned an engagement dinner for our family and friends. On the actual engagement day, Allen proposed to me with a ring. He did not get on one knee, but he managed to creatively leave me a list of notes with clues that led me to a restaurant where he was waiting for me, nervous, with the ring in my favorite drink. I was extremely excited about the ring because it was beautiful!

The engagement party was in October, and we planned to get married the following May. From then on, there were so many things to do to get prepared for the wedding. However, that did not change the dynamic of our relationship. Allen stopped staying out late and he started checking in more. He told me that he'd made a vow to God that we would be celibate until we said, "I do." I thought this was a bit weird because we had already had sex, but it made sense if God had told him to do this. He even went as far as not sleeping in the bed with me 90% of the time because it was "too tempting."

Preparing for the wedding went from excited to stressful. How in the world were we about to have a huge wedding when we were already struggling financially, and Allen was bad with money? Allen wanted a big wedding with outfit changes, complimentary drinks and a party bus. He wanted to host it at the largest arena in the city. We planned this huge, elaborate wedding that neither of us could afford. Our parents helped. Extended family helped. Sadly, the final check for the venue bounced. But we didn't find that out until after the wedding.

On our wedding day, we had family in town from all over the country. We had thirty-four people in the wedding party and an $800 additional bill before the reception could start. I cried the entire morning, but I couldn't explain my tears. I told everyone they were happy tears. I cried again at the altar. Perhaps my soul was saddened. Two months prior, I'd woke up from a deep sleep and I heard, "Wait!" I knew this was Holy Spirit speaking to me, but I couldn't wait. The wedding was basically around the corner. I prayed that God would fix all the things wrong with our relationship. I prayed that God would bring to pass all the confessions I spoke over my soon-to-be husband daily.

When the wedding was over, we had a terrible honeymoon in Florida that we couldn't afford. We stayed in the Extended Stay most of the time, creating struggle meals out of Ramen Noodles and sausages. I was looking forward to the honeymoon because, for the last seven months, I'd been celibate and fighting off urges to be intimate with my man.

My dreams were crushed on the first day of the honeymoon when he told me, "Just because we're married doesn't mean we have to have sex all the time."

Was he serious?

When we got back home, Allen went back to his normal behavior. He was gone all the time and didn't communicate.

One time, he told me he spent the night in jail after being pulled over by the police. However, I caught him in a lie because I was so worried about him that I called all the local hospitals and jails.

Allen made me believe that if we moved out of that house, he would be in a better space mentally. He was convinced that the house was filled with bad spirits from his past. Four months later, we moved into a rental in Flint. Allen suggested that we move to Flint because it was the halfway point between Bay City and Pontiac. It sounded good at the time.

We got settled into our new home, found a church home in the Flint area, and tried to create new healthy habits as a couple. This did not last long. Before I knew it, Allen was back to staying out late, lying about where he was going, and misusing money. In our new place, our bills doubled, and I had to carry the weight.

My attitude became cold toward Allen. He was back to sleeping on the couch and I attended our new church alone. In a matter of weeks, Allen lost his job, and his car broke down. He had been to every last-resort car lot between Bay City and Flint, and no one else would give him a car. He asked me to put a vehicle in my name for him. Although I did not want to, I did. We couldn't share a vehicle. I had too many memories of him being gone all night or having to "sleep in the car on the side of the road" because he'd caught a flat tire. I thought maybe he would be home more if he didn't have a car for a while.

During the time when Allen was unemployed, he was at home while I was at work. There were several times I came home, and it looked like the furniture was changed around. One time, I came home, and Allen had removed our wedding backdrop, all the wedding props on the wall, pictures of us, and even my shower gel from the bathroom. It was weird. However, the most disturbing part was the fact that Allen kept calling to ask me if I was home yet. He kept explaining that he'd rearranged a few things while cleaning up. When I saw what he had done, I didn't believe anything he said. I was certain he had someone in my house. Angry and frustrated, I waited for him to get home. When Allen walked through the door, we got into a heated argument, which led to him slashing all the tires on my truck.

A few weeks later, I received a call from Allen's cousin who had coordinated our wedding.

She said to me in a shaky voice, "You need to get a divorce."

I'd heard what she said, but my brain was not comprehending. With tears in her eyes, she explained to me that she heard something devasting about Allen. She believed it to be true. After being around Allen's family for almost two years, I'd learned that some of them were messy.

They had a habit of causing a scene. They even almost started a fist fight during our wedding rehearsal. I had to take this information with a grain of salt but keep it close to me. If it was true, it would come out.

I intentionally started arranging things in my home to see if Allen would move them while I wasn't there. About a month later, I went to church and my heart was heavy. I was tired of the stress, struggle and lack in my marriage. I cried the entire way to work that night.

I prayed to God, "Lord, if there's something I need to see, please show me."

Now, I would not advise anyone to pray this prayer unless you're ready for things to be exposed.

The next morning, I got off work early. I was supposed to work a double shift. Many times, throughout my shift, Allen called to ask what time I would be home. Something about the number of times he asked me that didn't seem right, so I felt like I should go home. I drove ninety miles per hour down the freeway to Flint, but I didn't know why I was speeding. I got a couple of texts from Allen on my way, but I did not answer. When I got to my street, I turned the corner and there was a car in my driveway. When I saw the car, I knew I was about to walk into something. I just wasn't sure *what or into whom I was walking.*

I pulled up to my driveway, but I parked at the end of it because I wanted to be able to leave quickly if I needed to. The unknown vehicle and my husband's vehicle were both running. I walked into the house. It seemed like my pictures were moved again. I didn't see or hear anyone, so I walked straight to my bedroom. When I got to the doorway, I saw Allen walking out of the bathroom, looking like he'd just seen a ghost. There was a man I didn't know sitting on my bed. Thank God this man was fully clothed, but he clearly did not know who I was, and he had *more attitude* than me.

I asked in a rude way, "Are you sleeping with my husband?"

Neither of them said anything. Everything after that was a blur, but I immediately got out of there. Before I left, I witnessed a small brawl, and my husband was the one being hit and cursed out. Allen did not say anything to the other guy about me or even try to defend himself in that moment.

"You can have him!" I yelled as I pulled off. Although Allen did not admit it, I saw it with my own eyes. He was gay or maybe bisexual. But he had been having a man in my home and often. Everything suddenly made sense. The letters I found in the old house. The empty lubricant bottles in his closet. The receipts for meals for more than one that were not for me. The phone records that he lied about.

I got out of Flint and went to my parents' house in Pontiac. I had to explain this story to my parents, my close friends, and to his parents, who seemed to have already known that he had a "past" that no one chose to share with me. That day was probably the most painful. I cried once. Then, I went into a depressive state. I wanted to sulk in my pain, but I had to pick myself up and make some tough decisions. The next day, I moved all my stuff out of the house, at least everything I could grab quickly. That was the last time I was there.

The divorce was just as tragic as all the other events. He left the state and would not peacefully agree to divorce. He even managed to bust the windows and rip the mirrors from my vehicle before he left. There had to be millions of calls to my job, my parents, threats and emails. After the longest two and a half years of my life, I can say I was married and divorced in 362 days.

By the time the divorce was final, I had already started my journey to happy, healthy and whole. The day the judge granted me the personal protection order was the first time I'd seen Allen since he'd damaged my vehicle. I could not look him in the eyes. When I walked out of that court room, I felt a freedom that was much like before I met him. It took all this time to realize that when I made the vow to refocus myself on God, soon after, I was easily distracted. I did not pray and ask God if this man was for me. Instead, I *assumed* He was the one for me because he seemed different.

A wise man once said, "Be careful of people who you think are so different that you have to ask God what "different" things they may be entertaining." When God woke me up out of my sleep and told me to wait, I did not listen. Because of my disobedience, I endured situations and circumstances I could have avoided.

When I reflect on all that I went through, I wish I would not have tilted my crown. But I am grateful for the lessons I learned. I would not be the woman I am today had I not went through that season. I learned many things about people, relationships, and, most of all, myself. After I got over the fact that I was twenty-five with a failed marriage from a relationship that was built on a lie, I could look in the mirror and tell myself, "It's not your fault."

I am much better after making it out of that marriage. I learned to listen to God when He speaks the *first time*. Now, I am eternally happy, healthy, whole and *recrowned*!

RECROWNING & Reflection

1. Why do you think women choose to ignore red flags in relationships?

   _____

   _____

   _____

   _____

   _____

2. How would you have reacted if you found your husband in bed with another man?

   _____

   _____

   _____

   _____

   _____

3. How would you help another woman heal who may be going through a situation similar to this?

ABOUT THE AUTHOR

Cierra Warren

She may not be able to change the world with a cake, but she can make it a better place by imparting a little love. Master baker and community influencer, Cierra T. Warren makes this her mission at the start of each new day. Cierra is a ten-year business owner who has worked diligently to build her business and brand. When she is not creating custom cakes, you can find her mentoring young adults in the community, teaching the importance of showing up for yourself, and helping others navigate through the challenges of life. Giving back to young adults is most important to Cierra having survived a disastrous divorce and many unexpected pivotal moments on her journey.

Cierra is well known in the community for her *Delicious Sweets*, as well as her humble spirit. She recently accepted a Young Professionals Award from the NAACP Saginaw Branch, where she was recognized for business and community leadership. Cierra has been featured in many articles in MLive, Saginaw News, and media interviews for Riverfront Saginaw and KISS 107.1.

Cierra shares her story for the first time in, *Recrowning God's Daughters*, an anthology featuring true stories from women who have proven to be resilient after defeat. The accomplished millennial describes her journey to getting over betrayal in marriage and becoming happy, healthy and whole.

To connect with Cierra, email ctwc404@yahoo.com.
To learn more about her baking business,
follow Delicious Sweets Bakeshop on Facebook and Instagram or browse the website at
www.dsibakeshop.com.

Pieces Of A Crown

Dr. Teresa B. Moore

I will never forget the day! February 3, 2016 was a brisk Monday morning in Michigan. The temperature had dropped during the night, and I was glad to have my thermals. The sun was shining outside, and the wind was blowing against my back as I hurried inside the building. Once inside, I was comforted by the warmth of the heat and the smile that greeted me in the foyer. A short older woman stood in front of me and asked me a question.

"Who are you here for?"

I paused momentarily and said, "Burrow." She pointed to the left hallway as she led me in that direction. I couldn't help but notice how I fumbled with my hands along the way. I felt like I was moving in slow motion as I walked toward the small waiting room. Inside the room sat my sister and brother. They both looked uncomfortable; we exchanged pleasantries. Then, we were all asked to go over into the next room. The atmosphere was dim. I froze as reality sunk in.

I was gazing down at the lifeless body of the woman who gave birth to me.

I was full of mixed emotions. Then, *it* happened. There was that familiar smell that flooded my nostrils. The first time I smelled "rotten chicken," or what I like to call the stench of death, was when I was sixteen years old. As I laid on a table, an older gentleman placed my feet in stirrups. My mother had authorized an unethical, illegal procedure for me.

She consented to terminating my baby, a six-month-old fetus.

"Open your legs! Scoot down! Relax!" These were the words he instructed me to do. I was shaking and afraid. The room was spinning as I shifted my eyes over to a crack in the wall. I tried my best to be still as I experienced what felt like my guts being ripped out of my body. I felt the speculum. Then, he inserted the needle. Next, I heard what sounded like suctioning. The pain was excruciating. I gripped the sides of the examining table. That awful smell of rotten chicken filled the air.

"Somebody, please help me! It hurts so bad!" I screamed. Tears fell from my eyes, and I was furious.

How could she do this to me? Again! I repeatedly told myself, "You're dreaming. Wake up."

Funny thing is I was *awake*. This was *not* a dream.

Moments later, I was in the recovery room. The walls felt like they were closing in on me. My heart was shattered into a million tiny pieces. *Am I dead yet?* I thought. Although I didn't physically die, I died on the inside with every step I took walking out of the clinic to my mother's boyfriend's car. There was an eerie silence inside the Cadillac. No one talked and neither of us moved. The next thing I remember is being shaken awake as the car pulled up to my grandmother's house.

"Go on in the house Tee and tell mama I will call her later," she instructed me to do. There was no hot meal, medication, hug or comfort for me. I was tossed out of the car like day-old trash. To make matters worse, I had to go on with life immediately, as if the abortion never happened. I was expected to, "Keep it moving."

I walked into grandmother's house as a hurting teen. I wanted *someone* to acknowledge my pain. But instead, I felt invisible. Nobody saw me. I headed straight to my sister's room to lie down. I went to sleep as a sixteen-year-old girl; however, I woke up as a bitter, broken sixteen-year-old girl. I wasn't allowed to weep for myself. Certainly, no one ever mentioned the abortion again—not my mother or any other family member.

The guilt, shame and torment I felt after witnessing the murder of my baby was beyond anything I could handle on my own. At a time when I should have been preparing to be "crowned" at my Sweet 16 birthday party with family and friends. There I was, replaying that dreadful day in my mind. I wondered if the baby would have been a boy or a girl. I wondered if he or she would have had thick eyebrows or almond-shaped eyes. I thought about what nickname I would have chosen. I wondered if he or she would grow into a healthy, happy baby and be a good student in school. Would he or she play sports or be class valedictorian? I never had a Sweet 16 party. There was no celebration. No one gave me a crown. Even if I had an imaginary crown, certainly, it was broken into pieces, just like I was.

My heart was hardened. Numbness and bitterness were the choice clothing I wore daily for many years. I was trapped emotionally, physically and mentally. The sixteen-year-old girl who walked into that clinic was not the same person who walked out. She never left the room of that abortion clinic. Instead, out walked an emotionally empty shell of a person.

It took some time for me to fully understand the impact of this loss. As difficult as it was, I survived. It was not an easy process to cope with the death of my baby. I didn't have the tools, nor was I allowed to go through the grieving process. To make matters worse, my boyfriend, nor his family, had a say in the matter. My mother made the decision for all of us. We were young kids in love. We never thought about the responsibility of raising a child. We were naïve and we thought we would be together forever. Our love was enough to weather any storm … or so we thought. We never stopped thinking about our baby.

Because I didn't receive therapy or support after the abortion, every area of my life was impacted negatively. I was a mess. It was only by the grace and love of God that I didn't lose my mind. I was a kid. I didn't know how to process what happened on that table. Although my mother had snatched life out of me, I had to put one foot in front of the other. Even though I wanted to die, I survived by choosing to get up every day and live. I would be lying if I said that it was easy. With every breath and step, I grew stronger. This is when the gathering of my crown started—the day I decided to push my feelings aside and pretend to move on.

Pretending came easily for me; I always dreamed of being rich and living in a good neighborhood with a white picket fence. I dreamed of being able to live a luxurious lifestyle with an excess of food, nice cars and unlimited shopping sprees. In my mind, this was the "good life." I was determined that, once I got from under my mother's roof, and out of the projects, I would never return. Pretending tainted every relationship I had. They were over before we even had a fair start. I couldn't accept someone loving me. *How could I?*

At birth, my father abandoned me. My mother killed any love I may have had inside of me on that dreadful day. Then, there was my boyfriend who was a drug dealer. He proclaimed to love me, but it was hard for me to believe since he couldn't keep his thirst for other women under control. So, moving through life emotionally unattached was my norm. I didn't become pregnant again until I was pregnant with my daughter, Cierra, at the age of eighteen.

This pregnancy started off rough. I had just been accepted into Florida A&M University. During my physical examination, I learned I was pregnant. I had a straight up temper tantrum! Every pinned-up emotion I had inside of me came bursting out. I was not going away to school. I was not going to be a doctor. I was going to be a mother. I sat staring at the nurse for what seemed like hours, crying, and trying to figure out how to tell my mother that I had failed her for the second time. I felt the air leave out of the examining room. I thought, *Oh, God! Why me?* Just when I thought I was finally getting away from my mother and the project life, here I was in a similar situation of having my choices being taken away from me.

The first time, my *mother* took away my right to be a mother. This time around, I made an irresponsible choice of having unprotected sex. Now, I was someone's mother. I vaguely remember the nurse's lips moving, but nothing she said registered with me. *Wait! Did she just say that I was twenty-one weeks pregnant?* Hearing this jolted me back to reality as I slid to the floor. I didn't have any time to waste. I had a baby coming soon and I needed to prepare.

If getting up off the floor was a challenge, then imagine the walk home from the doctor's office, which was all a blur to me. I can still see my mother with her glass of Crown Royal in her left hand and her Kool mild cigarette in her right as she looked at me with disgust. She made no excuses for her behavior or the language she used to express that she was not happy. *Again.* But this time around, she couldn't do anything about this pregnancy. Neither could I. To make matters worse, I went into labor in my sixth month. My body self-aborted one of the two fetuses! I was pregnant with twins and didn't even know it. My daughter Cierra was hiding on my left side. Doctors discovered this during an emergency ultrasound before a DNC.

However, her twin died. The abortion my mother consented to was now the reason that I would go into premature labor every time I reached six months in pregnancy. Talk about lasting effects. I was furious that her actions were, *once again*, causing me trauma. She had done enough damage to me to last a lifetime! The thought of losing another child was debilitating. I honestly didn't think I would survive another loss. The doctors did everything they could to preserve the life of my other baby. The blessing is that I was hospitalized six weeks later after my water broke. God saw fit to spare the life of a four-pound, ten-ounce baby girl born at twenty-seven weeks. He gave me a miracle and a second chance at life.

I visited church prior to giving birth. The pastor said that God loved me and that He would know I am His by the love I show to others. That message touched my heart. I knew within myself that I had to extend that love to my mother. Cierra's birth was the beginning of my forgiveness process with my mother and showing the love of Christ. I was nineteen years old when I delivered my daughter, but it wasn't until the age of twenty-two that I saw the effects of what healing looked and felt like.

In April of 1997, I accepted Jesus Christ as my personal Savior and joined a local church, which was the best thing I could do. God began to work in and through me as He restored my heart and the relationship between me and my mother. I was on the road to recovery and forgiveness was my first step toward freedom. However, there were times when the residue of my mother's choice resurfaced. For instance, God sent my husband to me when my daughter was just under the age of two. To our union, we birthed several children over the years. But during my sixth month, I always went into premature labor. I would literally be giving birth and praying to God that the baby would live, only to watch the child die in the arms of my husband. The pain, disappointment and lack of understanding I saw in the eyes of my husband sent my mind back to the age of sixteen.

Not only did my mother's decision affect me as a teen, but I was also still being affected by her actions as an adult. The difference during these times versus me being sixteen was that I now had a Savior who was ever present and holding and keeping me. I recited Isaiah 43:1 often, which is one of my favorite Scriptures: *But now thus says the LORD, who created me, and he formed me, and I don't have to fear for he has redeemed me, and he gave me his name.* I was God's chosen. His agape love for me blew my mind and helped empower me to get up and fight the good fight of faith. He was my sustainer and, with Him, I always triumph. With every loss, me and my husband grew closer. We trusted God even more. With every tear, God got the glory, and we never charged my mother for the loss.

Forgiveness is a choice! It is more than accepting an apology and moving forward. Forgiveness requires transparency with yourself and with others in order to move beyond your feelings and allow healing to take place. First, you must decide if you want to be healed from what has you bound. I knew that I didn't want to hate my mother forever; she was my mother, the person God chose to give me life. Although she wasn't perfect, she was my mother. I loved her, even if I did not like what she did. The Bible says in Matthew 6:14, *"For if you forgive other people when they sin against you, your heavenly Father will also forgive you."* One of the reasons I knew I had to forgive my mother was that I was now a mother. I wanted somewhat of a normal relationship with her for the sake of Cierra. So, I made the decision to look beyond me and my feelings and rebuild our relationship.

Cierra was the glue that held us together; however, our relationship had some major bumps along the way. I also had to take some responsibility in the role I played in my mother's decision to abort the baby. I had to ask myself some hard questions. *Why should my mother have to raise another kid that she didn't birth?* I never thought about the fact that we were poor, living in low-income projects with very scarce means. The decision she made was based on our situation, not on how either of us felt. Truth be told, my mother could barely keep her head above water. So, bringing another mouth into the household was not an option at the time.

I learned along my journey that forgiveness is allowing God's peace to piece us back together again. This was crucial on my road to healing. It was necessary that I was okay with not getting the apology. The fact of the matter is that my mother had moved on several years prior to me getting to this point, but I stayed stuck. This was a hard place to be in because I had been angry for so long that I couldn't see that I was trapped! *Was I choosing to stay stuck?* There had to be a mistake somewhere in my thinking because the Bible that I adapted to, and was now trying to live by, said in John 8:38, *So if the Son sets you free, you will be free indeed.* I knew I wanted this type of freedom, but I also wanted an apology from my mother. She needed to acknowledge that she was wrong!

Despite me wanting an apology, I never got it. I had to realize that she could only give me what was in her capacity. Thus, over time with the help of the Lord and a mental health therapist, I was able to release my mother and to grab ahold to freedom, along with God's peace, which surpassed my limited understanding. God's peace is not like anything I have experienced. I found it to be calming and protecting. For the first time in my life, I was embracing love and distancing myself from confusion. God had taken my broken pieces and He was making me whole with His peace.

For this to occur, we must be real with ourselves. We must give ourselves permission to feel, deal and heal. There is a misconception that once you are healed from something, there is no residue. It is perfectly okay to acknowledge feelings! Somewhere along the line, it appears to be an unspoken rule that there is a timeframe to feelings. We are only allowed to mourn, cry or be emotionally upset for a certain period of time. Every person is different, and each person must handle things their way, in their own time.

Forgiveness is using what God has placed inside of us to help others and allowing God to pull what is within us out. We are not our own; therefore, the struggles, hardships and afflictions we endure are to not only make us stronger—but to be used to build up others. God has well thought out plans for us. With these plans comes talents and giftings. We were created uniquely from one another; neither of us possesses the same imprint. Thus, our gifts are to edify and build up the body of Christ. Doing so helps us to take our minds off ourselves and our issues and focus on others' needs. When I did this, I was able to see past what was in front of me. I was able to assist someone else on their journey to navigating life. I also learned that forgiveness means being the solution to what I needed during my unforgiving posture. I needed someone to embrace me and to tell me that I was loved and cared for. So, I became what I needed. Supporting, encouraging and showing up for others became my priority. I didn't want anyone to experience the hell I'd endured on my watch. This encouraged me to become a licensed therapist.

Learning how to forgive others taught me that forgiveness is the choice to move beyond stuck people and go after hopes, dreams and goals, even if others never decide to move. Oftentimes, it's easier to complain and blame others. It's easier to use their actions to keep us at a standstill. The truth is that we have the option to move forward or not. I knew that I was created to do more, but it wasn't until my relationship with Christ was established that I really found out who I was and whose I was. Isaiah 43 reminds me that I am redeemed, that I was purchased by the Lord, and that He has given me His name! I came through the canal of my mother, but the Lord gave me His name after purchasing me. This is something to get excited about. With God on my side, I couldn't, and can't, lose. He was, and is, my champion! Knowing this helped me grow in Christ and embrace that I could do all things in Him because He gives me strength daily.

Another step in the forgiveness process is accepting that other people have the same choices and twenty-four hours a day that you have. Whatsoever they choose to do with them is not our concern. This means we need to stay in our lanes! We must embrace the fact that everyone is not "us." Everyone won't respond or do things the same way we do. Just because we are moved to do things a certain way does not automatically mean everyone will do things that way. This is where we can get our feelings hurt. We must accept that no two people are the same; we can only be concerned with how we do things. Whew! This almost took me out because I thought hearing my mother apologize would change my situation. What I really needed was a release to *live*. Forgiving my mother was never about me. Although she chose to hurt me, it was about living in right standing with God. It was in this place that I stopped complaining and started doing the work to—not just be right with God—but to use this journey toward forgiveness to activate my voice. True forgiveness is being vulnerable and open to be used in the area or areas of pain. Forgiveness and healing go hand in hand. It's one thing to forgive. But it's another thing to be *healed*.

Just like forgiveness, receiving God's healing is also a daily choice. We must arise daily and declare healing, as well as walk as though we are already healed. This is a challenge because the enemy is the accuser of the brethren; therefore, it is his job to make us doubt that we are healed. Healing looks different for each of us; however, we are God's workmanship and created in His image. Thus, in the healing process, we must allow the potter to mold us and come to accept that there may be some cracks in our design.

Learning how to forgive and receive God's healing opened the door of faith for me. I had watched God work in my life to help me forgive and I was embracing His healing, which strengthened my belief in Him. I knew that God was helping me. However, it wasn't until I read in Hebrews 11:6, *Without faith, it is impossible to please him, for whomever comes to God must believe.* I believed. Because of my faith in God, I was able to, through Him, grab ahold of my self-worth. I gave myself pats on the back!

My crown may have had fragmented pieces, but I gathered the courage to pick it up and place it on my head. I was no longer willing to be hostage to anyone or anything. I am the King's daughter and I been given permission to walk worthy of my calling. To do this, I had to stop being Holyfield's twin. I was beating up on myself and others! I put the gloves down and allowed God to love me as I loved on myself. I was gentle with myself and gave myself grace. I had endured some harsh realities that shaped the way I viewed things, so I needed to renew my mind. This happened when I let the Word wash my mind.

Ephesians 5:26 reminds us that God does not work apart from His Word; thus, if I truly wanted God to work in my life, I had to submit to His Word. Submitting to the will of God became my lifestyle. As a result, my relationship with my mother blossomed beautifully. We were best friends up until the day she died. My mother accepted Jesus Christ as her Savior and she lived a saved life. She served in her church, sang in the choir, and worked in the kitchen ministry. God restored her and made her whole right before my eyes. She did her best to live a life that was pleasing to God up until the day her assignment was finished here on earth. But one of the highlights of our relationship was when God showed me how much He loved me! He loved me so much that He allowed my mother and I to have a two-hour conversation. She told me all the things a daughter longed to hear from a mother.

Two hours later, she died.

So, there I was, staring down at my mother. The residue of the feelings I experienced on that tragic day so many years ago came rushing back to me as I prepared myself to say a final good-bye. I wanted to hate her. I wanted to make her relive my pain and sorrows. Yelling and screaming seemed appropriate. Yet, in that very moment, all I wanted was *my mommy*. I just wanted to hug her and tell her I loved her. I wanted to hear her laugh.

So, as I stood looking at her casket, I whispered, "I love you, Kakes!"

I adjusted my crown while nodding to Mr. Moon in approval for her body to be viewed by the public.

RECROWNING
& Reflection

1. How do you think getting counseling after the abortion would have affected me getting pregnant a second time?

   _____

   _____

   _____

   _____

   _____

2. Parents often make decisions for their children based on personal circumstances. How might this situation have been handled differently?

   _____

   _____

   _____

   _____

   _____

3. What are some necessary steps in the forgiveness process?

4. Do you agree or disagree that forgiveness and healing go hand in hand? Why? How?

ABOUT THE AUTHOR

Dr. Teresa B. Moore

Where others see destitution and despair, she sees hope, healing, and happiness. Affectionately known by many as The Purpose Pusher, Dr. Teresa B. Moore knows firsthand what it's like to deal with rejection, hurt and abuse. More importantly, she knows what it feels like to overcome that much and more. Strategic about helping others identify and change toxic behavior, her desire to see people happy, healed, and whole shines brightly for all to see—in and outside the four walls of the church.

As a community agent of change, minister and mental health professional, Dr. Moore takes pride in sowing seeds of hope and love throughout Pontiac, Michigan, and surrounding areas. As the owner and operator of Emages Counseling and Advocacy Services, she offers a variety of therapeutic services, including but not limited to individual, married and group counseling; assessments; and educational treatment services to clients and families in the time of crisis. She has over 29 years of extensive experience working with the developmentally disabled and mentally challenged population in various leadership roles. Holding both a Ph.D. in Religious Education, and a Master of Counseling, she prides herself on masterfully combining the Word of God with psychological processes and procedures to help her clients break free from past wounds and hurts that continue to hold them hostage.

In her work as an adjunct professor, Dr. Moore uses a connective instructional style called "Living Life with your Hands Wide Open." Serving in multiple capacities of help and customer service, she seeks to go above and beyond the normal call of duty—and encourages her students and mentees to do the same. Dr. Moore pinned her first book "*Awakened to Win*" in April of 2020. This book is filled with daily affirmations and prayer that is sure to jumpstart the day. She was included in *Gathering the Fragments* with her chapter "*Saved Junkie Looking Through Tainted Lenses*" in December 2020 and *Living and Loving Life Without Regrets* with her chapter "*Spilling the Tea*" in March 2022. Affiliated with numerous professional and community organizations, such as the American Counseling Association, *Psychology Today*, NOHS, HUS Club, the American Red Cross and Delta Sigma Theta Sorority, Inc., Dr. Moore is sure to bring life to any dead situation she encounters.

ABOUT THE AUTHOR–*Dr. Teresa B. Moore*

Having received the Professional Women's Club Shero Award twice, her creative ability to deliver resources, encouragement and strength to men and women who are at the end of their rope leads them to find their God-given purpose and passion. Whether she's hosting "Write the Vision! Work the Plan!" vision board workshop, or she's a participant in the annual "7-Up Service," attendees are sure to leave empowered and inspired to know that they are born with greatness within—they simply need to tap into it!

For more information or interviews, email dr.teresamoore@gmail.com or visit www.drteresamoore.com. Visit her on social media as DrTeresa Moore on Facebook or on Instagram as @dr.teresa_moore.

Weathering The Storms of Life While in Full Pursuit of My Purpose

Dr. Cherie Cofield

It was the beginning of the end. Life, as I'd come to know it for twenty-five years, had shifted and would never be the same.

It was May 8, 2016. My entire family was celebrating my late great-nephew's birthday. It should have been a happy, joyous occasion. But, when my oldest son arrived, he was acting, in a word, *different*. I later found out he was shooting steroids and drinking liquor, which sent him into a "steroid" rage—one that none of us could have prepared for.

My great-nephew got mad at my youngest son for no reason. So, my youngest son went outside. At the time, my youngest son weighed approximately 150 pounds, and my oldest son weighed approximately 250 pounds. My oldest son followed my youngest son outside, and they started fighting. My husband and I ran outside to intervene because he was too big to fight his little brother and it would cause division in the family.

Unfortunately, the commotion escalated to a major intersection, where my oldest son pulled a gun out.

"All of y'all gone jump me?" he asked, pointing the gun at my youngest son.

I was standing in front of my youngest son and my husband.

Before we knew it, my oldest son pulled the trigger. It was by the grace of God that the gun did not go off.

My husband had also raised my two older children from the time they were young kids. He was a "street guy" and he believed in street revenge. But he couldn't get back at my oldest son because he was conflicted. After all, we were married, and he had raised him.

Our relationship became strained after this, although we'd never had a great marriage. My husband began drinking much more excessively. This caused even more problems. He was literally drunk all the time, and he never wanted to talk to me. I was also a second-year Ph.D. student at the time. I could not focus on my husband or his drinking, so I decided to put myself first. Little did I know making myself a priority was causing more harm than good.

In November of 2016, my husband celebrated his fiftieth birthday. That weekend, he decided to spend the weekend away without any communication. When he returned home, I was livid, to say the least.

"Pack your bags!" I told him. "Go right back to wherever you have been all weekend because it's obvious that's where you wanted to be!"

He cried. He apologized to our son and me. He told me that he still wanted our marriage to work. He offered to change his shift at work from midnight to days and quit drinking. He even said he would stop hanging out with the motorcycle club. He also suggested that we attend counseling, and he admitted that he had many unresolved issues from his childhood. We had a heart-to-heart conversation. We were honest about what we both needed in the marriage. I never felt closer to him than at that moment.

I agreed to stay.

He had never apologized or cried about *anything* in our marriage.

Surely, *this time*, he was sincere.

"If you stay out again, our marriage is over," I told him.

After he went to work, our son said, "Mom, he isn't going to stop."

In February 2017, the inevitable happened. He did *it* again. He went to work on February 18, at 5 p.m. for his 7 p.m. to 7 a.m. shift. I did not hear from him until after I got home from church the following day. My phone rang. When I saw it was him calling, I had an instant attitude.

"What are you doing?" he asked, sounding happy, but inebriated.

"What do you mean what am I doing? I am just getting home from church!"

His friendly sound instantly changed. He said, "I am on my way home." He hung up the phone, but he did not come home. I called his phone several times without an answer, which angered me even more. I texted him, "Stay where you are. It's over!"

When he returned home, on February 20, 2017, he was in the shower when I walked in the door from work. He acted as if nothing had happened.

I immediately asked him, "Why are you here?"

He said, "I thought we could talk."

"We have nothing to talk about! We are done! Go back to wherever you came from!"

He didn't even attempt to mumble a word. He simply packed his belongings and left.

Our son said, "Mom, I don't know why you gave him another chance. I told you he wasn't going to stop."

Our son appeared sad, but relieved. He'd watched our rocky relationship all his life.

I had not spoken to my oldest son since May of 2016. But once he heard about me moving and getting a divorce, he immediately texted me. "I just wanted to let you know that I am sorry for what's going on and, if you need me, I am here for you. I do admire the fact that you hung in there, like a wife is supposed to, through it all. I saw you lose it all and get it all back while carrying the load on your shoulders. I am very proud of you and how you are a fighter." This allowed my oldest son and I to reconnect.

My sons and friends helped me moved out of our marital home on March 6, 2017, and I filed for divorce on March 7, 2017. It was my birthday present to me. I didn't talk to my husband or see him until June of 2017, when his father passed.

The first time we spoke to each other or saw each other since the divorce filing was at his father's viewing. We hugged and I expressed my sympathy. We stood at the casket and had general conversation. After I sat down, his girlfriend walked in. Soon, he and my son went outside and started arguing. My son could not believe how disrespectful his father was, but I was not surprised by then. I walked outside to stopped them from fighting. My ex-husband was angry. I did not understand why.

He said, "You never called me or tried to contact me."

I replied, "I gave you what you wanted."

He was intoxicated.

After his father's funeral, we briefly spoke again.

I apologized. He apologized, as well.

I thought that chapter of my life was closed. But I couldn't have been more wrong.

My ex-husband turned into a monster after his father passed. He began to show his true colors ... or ... should I say, his mask fell off. I saw the *real* him. He prolonged the divorce process for more than a year. He didn't want to help support our adult depressed son, although he was the cause of his depression. He didn't want to pay alimony, although we agreed that I would stop working to further my education. He even wanted the stainless-steel appliances, although I'd purchased them with my retirement funds. He fought me on everything because he wanted to walk away scot-free. I was in total disbelief because he used to always say, "If we ever break up, I will walk away without anything and start over."

Our divorce was final on our son's birthday, May 8, 2018. Ultimately, my ex-husband sold our home for less than what it was worth so he wouldn't have to give me any money. He didn't have to pay off any of our debt we incurred during our marriage, including the truck that I purchased so we could start a business. He was only ordered to pay a portion of my student loans when I finished school.

Most days after my divorce, I did not know where my next meal was coming from or if I would have a roof over my head. All I could do was put one foot in front of the other. I was so close to homelessness I could taste and smell it. All I could do was cry out to God and pray. God sent me a couple of "angels." One paid my rent and bought me groceries. The other gave me money to get my hair styled.

I started counseling and soon realized that I had laid down my crown the moment my ex-husband said, "I do not like for my women to wear make-up."

That didn't bother me because I did not wear it at the time. That was the beginning of the pruning process. I voluntarily agreed to anything he said. But once I agreed to that, the crap began to flow without hesitation. The disrespect started, and I found out I was pregnant. I did not want to raise another child as a single parent, and I told him so. That was my first mistake. I told him my weakness and he used it to his advantage. He cheated on me, lied to me, abused me mentally and emotionally, and assaulted me once to the point where I ended up with a broken wrist.

Throughout the marriage, he would spend the night out and blame it on being drunk. For too long, I believed him. He often came home so drunk that I would wonder how he made it home. One time while at a friend's funeral, he drank so much that when he went to stand up, he fell out. So, seeing him drunk was not unusual; it was something he did often.

If we were invited out, we would not leave until he was drunk or all the liquor was gone, no matter how I felt. Many times, I was exhausted or had to go to work the next day. However, that did not matter to him. I was always his designated driver.

I realized that I had given him all power over me by relinquishing my crown. Life, as I knew it, would never be the same. I was no longer in control of my life; I was being controlled mentally. Before getting married, I was independent and smart. I never took anything from a man. So, I do not know why I accepted everything he dished out.

Divorce counseling taught me a lot about myself. I learned that I gave everyone *everything* and forgot about myself in the process. I discovered this started as a child. I was the last of four children. I always needed to be liked and loved. I gave to my ex-husband, my children, and anyone who asked for anything, even when I did not have it to give.

I also discovered that my marriage mirrored my mother's and stepfather's relationship. My stepfather was an alcoholic who took care of home but liked to hang out when drinking. My mother ignored him. He would buy her something, then they would be good again. I realized I did the same thing in my marriage. I also learned that I was never happy in my marriage, and I used food and liquor as comfort.

During counseling, I discovered that I never saw a productive marriage or never had a role model of a wife. Even my grandparents on my mom's side had a dysfunctional marriage filled with cheating. My grandmother accepted it.

How could I be a wife if I never saw what a wife looked like in everyday life? Counseling allowed me to learn who I was. It also allowed me to learn what I want, what I will not accept, and what I deserve in a marriage. I deserve to be loved like Christ loved the church.

While I was in the storm, I thought it would never pass. I cried out to God and asked, "Why me, Lord? Why do I have to endure all this pain?"

In the midst of trying to process my new normal throughout the divorce process, I had to focus on my classwork and furthering my education. I wanted to quit—*too many times to count*. I endured a lot of criticism, mental and emotional abuse, divorce, bankruptcy, prohibited career progression, being looked over, job loss, medical illness, and mental/emotional distress. I suffered from imposter syndrome, and I was purposefully being led astray. I was pushed to the back repeatedly. But I knew I had to keep pressing forward, despite the obstacles. Someone told me that I had to press on because what I was going through was—not just for me—but for those who will come behind me.

During one of my clinicals, God told me why.

He said, "I chose you because I knew you could handle it."

He also knew that I would show his daughters that they could survive divorce and school, as well. One day during my clinical, I was being transparent with my students. I told them about my divorce and challenges with school. Before I could finish my story, one student began to cry.

She told me, "I questioned why I failed my class last semester and was asking God why? I received my answer through your story today. I failed the class because I was supposed to meet you."

She immediately started thanking God. Before I knew it, we were all praising God and crying. I was crying because I got my answer, as well. I have been told many times that it has been a blessing to see a Black woman who has overcome adversity and still be able to pursue your purpose, in spite of divorce. Many students told me, "I know I can do it because God did it for you."

As I continued to pursue my degree, the attacks continued. Soon, COVID-19 hit. I found myself in a bind once again. I asked God again, "Why me?". I was presented with an opportunity to pivot my nursing career to become a Cannabis Nurse Consultant. I would be able to use my nursing degree in the newly approved medical marijuana law in Michigan. I would be able to consult, educate and follow cannabis patients on the safe consumption of cannabis. Little did I know that this would align with my theory of using alternative and complementary medicine (mindfulness).

I signed up for the class and my life changed once again. Once it was announced that I'd signed up for the Cannabis Nurse Consultant class, I received over one hundred telephone calls and text messages from all over the United States asking about products. After learning about Cannabidiol and its therapeutic effects without getting high, I knew this was where I was supposed to be. I did the leg work and started my own brand of premium CBD products. This resulted in the birth of 2C CannaHealth and Wellness, LLC, an ecommerce business. I developed a mission for my business venture. My mission is to offer education, health, and wellness in a holistic way to relieve pain nonpharmacologically (no medication) to anyone with a chronic disease without side effects, to assist with bringing the body back into balance/ homeostasis. I was soon helping many people find, "Relief without the High."

Ultimately, when you find yourself weathering life's storms in the midst of pursuing your purpose (and if you haven't yet, you most definitely will), keep these tips in mind that helped get me to the other side in one piece:

1. **Find your support system.** If your circle doesn't consist of people who can empower you when times get tough, create a new circle. It may not be ten people. You may only have two people in your circle you can truly depend on and trust. Cultivate the relationship with those two. When I went through my divorce, the Lord replaced the man I lost with ten male cousins and friends. They stepped up to the plate and showed me what real love from a man looked like. Some of them still call and check on me. They spent quality time with me and told me that I was special and beautiful when I didn't feel like any of that. They were genuine in their approach, and they never asked for anything in return. Create your tribe and lean on them until you are strong enough to stand on your own.

2. **Join a prophetic church.** Without my church family, I'm not sure where I'd be. Without the powerful teachings of my co-pastor, and the connection of like-minded

individuals, I was able to build hope and faith for the future. Find a ministry where you can grow spiritually and mentally. You may even find part of your support system in your church family. Just like you feed your body food every day, you need to be fed spiritually. This was my foundation in those times when I felt like the very ground beneath me was sinking. You are not in this alone. There is power in community.

3. **Strengthen your prayer life.** Quite simply, prayer is simply communication with the Creator. Don't overcomplicate it or make it a monologue. You don't have to kneel beside your bed. You don't even have to close your eyes. Speak as if you are talking to a long-time friend, seeking a solution to a problem. You can pray in your car, at your desk at work, or even while you're walking around your neighborhood. It's not a chore; it's a conversation. Say what you need to say, but don't forget to listen for the answer or the strategy. Many people don't pray effectively because they never leave time and space to receive an answer.

God removed one, but He put many real men in my life who showed me what it meant to be loved. I was connected to approximately ten male cousins who stepped up to the plate and showed me true love, some of which I had never met face-to-face. They called and texted to check on me frequently. I never missed my previous relationship because of the support and attention these men showed me, by the grace of God.

Today, I'm *Doctor* Cofield and I work at the University of Michigan, University of Detroit Mercy, and many other institutions in the metropolitan Detroit area. In the midst of it all, God restored to me more than what I thought I'd lost.

According to James 1:12 (NIV), *Blessed is the one who perseveres under the trial because, having stood the test, that person will receive the crown of life that the Lord has promised to those who love him.*

Amid the adversity, I completed my Ph.D. in Nursing degree. My Ph.D. research study is groundbreaking in adolescents with chronic pain from sickle cell disease (SCD) that participate in a mindfulness martial arts program. The purpose of this study was to explore the experience of adolescents with chronic pain from SCD who were attending the Kids Kicking Cancer mindfulness martial arts program in Southfield, Michigan, and its potential for helping alleviate their pain. This is the first-time chronic pain, function and perceived control over pain is being studied in this patient population. I have participated in several conferences and presented a poster on my research.

God gave me so many jobs that I could not accept them all. I was also able to start a successful Cannabidiol (CBD) business. I am a Cannabis Nurse Consultant, educator, advocate, and speaker on the safe consumption of cannabis. I have been a guest panelist speaking about cannabis on many online forums, as well.

I never dreamed that the Lord would take me from the back to the front.

According to Matthew 19:30, *But many who are first will be last, and the last first.*

I am making more money than I ever have in my life. I am living a life of healing, wholeness and abundance. If God did it for me, he can do it for you. God is so good to me, and He is not done yet.

Life is a series of putting out fires and weathering storms. You don't know when the storm is going to come, nor how long it is going to last. One thing is certain: storms will come. It's how you respond to them that makes the difference between life and death, the beginning or the end.

RECROWNING & Reflection

1. When did you take your crown off in your relationship?

   _____

   _____

   _____

   _____

   _____

2. What was your support system like during times of trouble?

   _____

   _____

   _____

   _____

   _____

3. How do you think you can weather a storm in pursuit of your purpose?

ABOUT THE AUTHOR

Dr. Cherie Cofield

In spite of divorce and other challenges faced during Cherie's Ph.D. studies, she's held a 3.78 GPA. Cherie holds a Bachelor, Master, and Ph.D. degree in Nursing. Cherie is a role model for women who are going through or have gone through divorce to show them that they will make it through successfully. She is living proof that if you keep putting one foot in front of the other, there is success on the other side of divorce.

Cherie has endured criticism, mental and emotional abuse, divorce, bankruptcy, prohibited career progression, being looked over, job loss, medical illness and mental/emotional distress. She has also suffered from imposter syndrome, purposefully been led astray, and been pushed to the back. In spite of it all, God restored it all. She does not look like what she has been through.

Cherie has won several awards while pursuing her Ph.D. She was the first recipient of the Wayne State University King Chavez Parks Future Faculty Fellowship Award in the School of Nursing and the recipient of the Wayne State University Rumble Fellowship Award. Cherie belongs to the National Hemp Association and the American Cannabis Nurses Association. Cherie is an active community servant with many religious organizations in metropolitan Detroit, serving the homeless, as well as mentoring many nursing students.

For booking or speaking engagements, visit www.2ccannahealthandwellness.live or email cheriecofield@2ccannahealthandwellness.live.
You can also connect with Cherie on Instagram @iceco_38 or Facebook @Cherie Cofield PhD.

The Prodigal Daughter

Tenita C. Johnson

I sat on the edge of the bed, thinking to myself, *What in the hell did I just do?* Literally.

For a moment, I wished, I hoped, I prayed it was simply a bad dream that I had awakened from. But soon, I realized I had done the unthinkable and the unimaginable. I got up and showered, trying to wash the stench of filth off of me. I knew I'd made a huge mistake, but I didn't know how to fix this one. Hell, I didn't even think it was possible to fix this one. I packed my bags and prepared to drive home from a long weekend in Chicago with family and friends. I had a lot to think about on the four-hour drive.

But there's one thing that never crossed my mind: *telling my husband.*

✳ ✳ ✳ ✳ ✳

Approximately two weeks prior to this earth-shaking weekend in Chi-Town, my husband and I had some type of argument. As usual, at the time, we did what we always did when we had a disagreement. We stopped talking for days, which then turned into weeks. He slept on the couch while I slept in the bedroom. We did our best not to cross paths in the house. We slammed cabinets in the kitchen and slammed doors when we entered or exited the house, so the other person didn't have to guess about where we were—physically, emotionally and spiritually. All communication ceased besides a few text messages regarding finances or the children. Even if we did attend church back then, during a time like this, we went to church in separate cars and entered the church at opposite ends of the building. We didn't say "Good morning" or "Good night" for too many days to count. So, I naturally went into fight-or-flight mode. Honestly, I was tired of fighting. Therefore, that only left me one option: *flight*.

I was considerate enough to wake my husband at 6 a.m. on a Saturday morning to let him know I'd be traveling to Chicago for the weekend. I wasn't looking for a response. But, of course, he had one prepared.

"While you're there, you need to decide if you really want this marriage. I need an answer when you get back."

I responded simply by walking out the side door, getting into my vehicle and driving down I-94 for four hours. I cried the whole way as I talked to several friends on the phone en route to my destination. You see, we'd been married for ten years. We attended regular Marriage Sunday School classes at our church, and we even had numerous marital counseling sessions with our Sunday School teachers. Many couples who had been married much longer than us always told us, "Once you get past the first five years, it's smooth sailing." They couldn't have been more wrong. It was ten—not five—years later, and, unfortunately, we still found ourselves at the same spot at least once a year: *preparing for divorce*. If he didn't threaten to leave me, I threatened to leave him. If he didn't go over to his brother's house to get away, I ran away to a friend's house who would let me and my son stay until things cooled off. We literally said, "I'm done and I'm out!" so many times that I stopped counting. It was our go-to statement to shut down every argument and misunderstanding. Little did we know just how powerful those words really were at the time.

When I made it to Chicago, I immediately went to my cousin's home, which is where I stayed most times when I visited. As always, many of my cousins met me at the house for a time of laughs, food and fun. But understand that these cousins are not saved. So, alcohol and weed were also thrown into the mix. I was used to their habits and, at the time, it didn't bother me. I just needed to get away for the weekend to clear my head and heart from all the hurt. I was tired of going around the same mountains and cycles with little to no victory. Clearly, something was wrong, and we didn't know how to fix it—if it *could* be fixed. My intention was to party, drink a bit, enjoy my best life for the weekend, and drive home late Sunday evening. I was definitely running away from my problems. But nothing could have prepared me for what—and who—I was running *toward*.

My cousin Drake invited his friend Sean over for the family festivities. After all, they'd been friends since they were little kids on the block. Drake and Sean were more like brothers than friends. I knew Sean had a crush on me when he was younger, but it had been years since I'd seen him in person. Sean arrived at the house that Saturday at noon and my cousins had already started drinking. After all, they didn't need a special occasion or a specific time on the clock for permission.

As we sat around the house most of the day, Sean started what I considered casual conversation. But after a while, he went a bit deeper.

"I heard you lost twin babies. I'm so sorry for your loss."

How did he know that?

"I saw you wrote a book! I'm proud of you! Congratulations! That's such a huge accomplishment!"

I thought to myself, *Dang! For somebody who lives in another state, this man has definitely been keeping tabs on me from afar!*

I was flattered. I was impressed. I felt loved. I felt special. What I didn't recognize was that I was vulnerable. The more we talked, the more I backed myself into a corner. When we rode to drop Drake off at home, Sean and I got pulled over. Little did I know, he had a gun and drugs in the van. He also had an expired license. I had left my purse at the house, so I didn't have any identification on me. I was terrified that the police would take us both to jail. Fortunately, and unfortunately, they told me I could drive the van home. But he couldn't drive it because of his suspended license.

Strike one.

When we got back to my cousin's home, she told me all of the female cousins were preparing to go to a couple of parties. I hadn't packed party clothes and I didn't feel like putting on makeup. And, quite frankly, I was enjoying the hours of deep conversation with Sean. My cousins begged me to go. They even offered to let me wear some of their clothes and they volunteered to do my makeup. But I wasn't feeling pretty at the moment. After helping them pick out their stellar outfits, I declined for the final time. Before I knew it, it was 10 p.m. and they were heading out the door for a night out on the town—*without me.*

Strike two.

At this point, Sean and I were the only two left at the house. All of my male cousins had gone home, and my female cousins went to the party as a group. We continued talking well into the late night. He told me he wasn't happy in his marriage, so he had separated from his wife. He told me they were in the middle of a divorce. Even though she still wanted the marriage, he was done with her. Ironically, I was *done*, too. I was *done* fighting. I was *done* trying. I was *done* crying. I was *done* going around in circles with someone who clearly didn't love me or want me. I was *done* losing sleep. I was *done* with walking around the house for weeks, not speaking. I was *done* with being ignored in my own home. I was *done* being tolerated, but not celebrated. In that moment, I didn't feel like I had anything to lose. In my mind, in my heart, my marriage was over. Whatever was left of it wasn't enough to rebuild. I had reached the point of no return—emotionally and physically.

Suddenly, there was an unexpected knock on the door. It was my drunk cousin, Jared. His friends had dropped him off at my cousin's house because he was too wasted to drive himself home. We laid Jared on the couch and tried to help him sober up quickly. We gave him some water and a

Stanback so he wouldn't have a hangover. But, for the most part, he wasn't coherent. He started dancing wildly. He told us repeatedly that he loved us. He even vomited a few times. Within an hour or so, he was passed out on the bed in the spare bedroom at the back of my cousin's house and we couldn't wake him up until the next morning.

Strike three.

At this point, I felt like I was out of options. I didn't have anything else to lose. I had already lost in the game of marriage, and I didn't want to play again. So that night, I voluntarily laid my crown down. I left it somewhere downstairs. I'm not even sure where or when. But when I went upstairs, I was *crownless*.

There was no morning-after pill for the damage I'd done that night. I couldn't undo what I had done. Waking up to the reality that I'd had a one-night affair on my husband was almost debilitating. I literally felt like my soul had left my body. I felt dirty. Tainted. Stained and blemished, almost to the point where I was unrecognizable. God has warned me not once, but three times before I'd voluntarily laid my crown down and laid with a *pig*. Not only was he married, but he had multiple children, and he sold drugs on the streets of Chicago. He didn't have a *real* job. He didn't wine and dine me at Ruth's Chris or Morton's Steakhouse. He hadn't bought me lavish gold or jewelry. I was capable of being easily lured to him simply because he spoke my love language—words of affirmation—and my husband wasn't speaking to me at all.

In Luke 15:11-16, *Jesus shares this parable: "There was once a man who had two sons. The younger said to his father, 'Father, I want right now what's coming to me.'* "*So the father divided the property between them. It wasn't long before the younger son packed his bags and left for a distant country. There, undisciplined and dissipated, he wasted everything he had. After he had gone through all his money, there was a bad famine all through that country and he began to feel it. He signed on with a citizen there who assigned him to his fields to slop the pigs. He was so hungry he would have eaten the corncobs in the pig slop, but no one would give him any.*

In a moment, I had traded my crown for pig slop.

The following week was tumultuous, to say the least. I still had no intention of telling my husband about the whole ordeal—until God told me I had to. I returned from Chicago late Sunday. I didn't get up the nerve to tell him until Friday, two days before Father's Day. I surely was not about to tell him alone either. He had never laid a hand on me or hit me. But I was almost certain that I'd at least end up in a chokehold for this one.

I scheduled an appointment at our church with our then marriage counselor. We didn't drive to the church together and that was intentional on my part. I wasn't even sure I'd be able to feel safe enough to go home after I told him what I needed to tell him—let alone ride home with him afterward. In our meeting, my counselor spoke most of the time at first to preface what I was about to tell him. I could only muster up a few words because of the heavy shame, guilt and fear.

"I stepped out of the marriage," I murmured.

That one statement was followed by a series of questions from him—not just that night—but for months to come.

With who? When? Were you drinking and smoking? How many times? How long has this been going on?

Thinking that he had a "right" to know as many details as he felt like he needed to know, I simply answered every question to the best of my ability. He sped out of the church parking lot and left me there with our marriage counselor. He told me it was over and that he was done. This time, I believed him. Even my counselor told me, "Men can cheat, and women forgive them. Women cheat, and it becomes a different story. Men can't handle that."

I was relieved in a sense. A boulder of fear of how he would respond was lifted. But for safety reasons, I stayed with a friend that night instead of going back to the house. Just like Jesus Christ's story, Friday looked hopeless. He'd packed up half of the house and said he was moving out. He told me he would file for divorce and would simply tell family and friends that we had irreconcilable differences. Even in my mess, he was willing to cover up for me. I'm sure he didn't want to endure the shame of being cheated on by his wife either. I had laid my crown down and made my bed. I had to lie in it. I slowly came to grips with the consequences.

But Sunday, somehow, the story flipped. He asked if he could pray for me and with me. He told me that he forgave me, and he wanted to make the marriage work. He apologized for leaving me "uncovered" and not speaking to me for weeks. We weren't out of the woods yet, though. The next six to eight months were hell on earth for me. He kept asking me questions and he expected me to give him an answer at the drop of a dime. We rode the seesaw of him leaving vs. him staying. We rode the seesaw of getting a divorce or simply separating to repair the marriage. I even moved out for three months and had my own apartment. At some point, I had to get off the seesaw of emotions with him, even though I was the cause of the onset of the chaos.

Six months later, he, too, traveled and had an affair. I laughed. I was almost relieved. That's what I expected him to do. It just took him some months to do it. I wish I could tell you that one thing saved our marriage. Yes, we attended a Marriage Bootcamp, which we serve as teachers for now.

We've both had some form of individual counseling. We've hosted marriage small groups and attended marriage small groups. We've prayed a lot. We've fasted a lot. We've still wanted to quit *a whole lot*. In October of 2022, we celebrate nineteen years of marriage. It's nothing but the grace of God that we've been through so many storms and fires, and we're still standing.

This whole experience taught me a few things. The first thing it taught me was not to judge anyone else. Matthew 7:2 says, *For in the same way you judge others, you will be judged, and with the measure you use, it will be measured to you*. Just a week before I laid my crown down in Chicago, I was criticizing another woman at my church who was openly cheating on her husband. It was so much easier to say what I would *not* do when it wasn't me. I learned very quickly how the tables often turn.

The second thing the affair taught me was that God always sends a warning. Psalm 34:19 (ESV) says, *Many are the afflictions of the righteous, but the LORD delivers him out of them all*. I had many ways of escape. I had chosen to ignore the blaring warning sign when the police stopped us, when my cousins asked me to go to the parties, and when my drunk cousin landed on our doorstep. I had ways out. I could never say that God didn't forewarn me and try to redirect me.

The third lesson I learned was that the enemy knows just what you like, even more than you or your spouse may know. He knew I needed to be affirmed. I wanted to be affirmed. In my weakness, I was attracted to anything and anyone that could, and would, affirm me. After being rejected so many times through life, I've learned that words truly hold a lot of power for me—good or bad. So, when a male tells me he's not only sorry for the loss of my children, but that he's also been keeping up with my author journey—and even read some of the book—it left me wide open.

The fourth lesson I learned was that my husband truly loves me as Christ loves the church. I had many family members who told me he would, and should, divorce me. My counselor told me he would leave me. Many other ministerial leaders I consulted told me not to even tell him—if I wanted to keep my marriage anyway. Some of my friends told me to simply go through with the divorce without telling him about the affair because, at that point, our marriage was over.

And, in a word, it was *over*. We couldn't continue to do the same things we'd always done. We couldn't continue to keep arguing over the same issues. We couldn't continue to walk around our home, not speaking for days that turned into weeks. Marriage, as we knew it, was, unfortunately, but thankfully, *over*. Something, or someone, had to interrupt the pattern. We didn't like the way this chapter of our lives played out. It was rough and emotional. It was exhausting and painful. But, in the process of healing and revival, I gained a new respect and a new love for my husband. While he may have lost some respect for me, I like to believe that this season also showed him what it's like to lose me. The truth is, long before that weekend in Chicago, I had mentally moved out.

The final thing this season taught me was that divorce is an option—not a must—after infidelity. Many people say it's their deal-breaker, and it's the one thing they can't forgive. But I know firsthand that there is *nothing* that can't be forgiven. It's all a matter of choice and deciding. If you've already made up your mind to leave, you will leave physically after an affair. If you've already made up your mind that this is grounds for divorce, you will immediately get a divorce. But you don't *have* to. The two people in the marriage still have free will to choose. If I know nothing else, I know God can not only restore—but rebuild a marriage *better*—after infidelity. He didn't cause it. But He can sure use it for His glory!

Like the prodigal son, I am restored and redeemed. I now know who I am and whose I am. I am a daughter of the King, a daughter of the Most High, and I don't have to settle for pig slop!

RECROWNING & Reflection

1. What's one instance where God gave you a warning, but you ignored it?

   _____
   _____
   _____
   _____
   _____

2. In your opinion, how can infidelity *help* a marriage?

   _____
   _____
   _____
   _____
   _____

3. Where did you lay your crown down in the past?

4. What was the restoration process like to get your crown back?

5. What would you say to empower and encourage a woman who has lost her crown to infidelity?

ABOUT THE AUTHOR

Tenita C. Johnson

Transforming pain into purpose is a gift that authorpreneur, speaker and book coach, Tenita "Bestseller" Johnson gives to everyone she encounters. She is a warrior of words with a fierce passion for guiding authors to expand their brand by showing them how to earn multiple streams of income from just ONE book. As the author of 18 books, seven of which have been Amazon bestsellers, she is living proof that sharing your story leads to your destiny.

Familiar with rising from numerous fires and coming out unscathed, Tenita has triumphed over suicidal thoughts, depression, low self-esteem, marital storms and blended family woes. She has also endured miscarriages and the stillbirth of twins the day after she married her husband. Each of these tragedies has added indelible layers to her resilience. With more than 25 years in journalism, writing and editing, she has a knack for creating narratives that are authentic and raw, yet endearingly relatable. She is a vessel with the ability to change lives and impact the world, thus she is a proud "book bully," who relentlessly urges others to, "Write the book and get paid for the pain!"

When Tenita speaks, people listen with their ears as well as their hearts and souls because her transparency transcends pretense. She is a bold beacon of hope who inspires others to seek their highest peak. One of her proudest and defining moments was her appearance on Kirk Franklin's Praise Sirius XM channel.

As the founder and CEO of So It Is Written Publishing, she has helped hundreds of authors birth their books in record time. The 12-year-old company excels as a one-stop shop for the complete book process from conception to completion, not just editing. The editorial guru successfully helps people to pen books that will boost their brand, accelerate their paydays and bust open doors of endless opportunities. So It Is Written won The Sunrise Pinnacle Award for Diversity Company of the Year, in 2020, from the Rochester Regional Chamber of Commerce in Rochester, Michigan. For six years, Tenita hosted the Red Ink Conference in Atlanta, Detroit, Charlotte and Chicago. Over 600 attendees received invaluable information from industry leaders on how to write, edit, market and publish their next bestseller.

Beyond her books, her versatility shines in multiple areas, including her role as the executive producer of the hit stage play, *When the Smoke Clears*, which was based on her book, *When the Smoke Clears: A Phoenix Rises*. The play ran in 2017 and 2018 to sold-out audiences in downtown Detroit. She also served as the editorial director for *Career Mastered Magazine* and *Hope for Women Magazine*. Currently, she is the national president of The Aspiring Writers Association of America, a writers' organization that works with writers worldwide to pen their next literary masterpiece.

Tenita's passion for delivering bestselling books is matched only by her devotion to helping women and men heal from the drama, trauma and baggage of sexual abuse. Her 2021 anthology, *HUSH: Breaking the Cycle of Silence Around Sexual Abuse*, features eight women who lost their innocence and identity to life-altering trauma. She is a huge advocate and mouthpiece for those who have been sexually abused as she empowers them to release their pain instead of suffering in silence.

Her future plans include the release of *HUSH III*, producing her short film *What Happens in This House*, and completing the script for her feature film *When the Smoke Clears*. As a catalyst for positive change, she is a woman who has learned to live an intentional life of purpose while unapologetically fulfilling her God-driven assignments.

For booking or speaking engagements, email info@soitiswritten.net or visit www.tenitajohnson.com.

Unveiled

Dr. Kathleen Abate

Sometimes, life's most pivotal moments, the moments that actually change the trajectory of our lives, happen at the most unexpected time, in the most unexpected place. Thinking back on the most pivotal moment in my life brings to mind a memory so vividly clear that I almost can't believe seventeen years have passed since it happened. It feels like it was just yesterday. It's a funny thing how the mind works.

For most of us, we live each day without even thinking about the fact that we probably won't remember every detail of the day in a week. Most of the day will be completely forgotten, almost erased. With 365 days in a year, think about how many days you've already lived and how many of all of those days you actually remember in detail. Not many, right? When we really think about it, the majority of our past is completely forgotten, almost as if it never even happened. But every one of us has those few unforgettable moments sprinkled throughout our lives that remain imprinted in the depths of our memory forever, no matter where we are or what we're doing. They're the moments that stand out to us. Moments that instantaneously changed us, either for better or worse. In all actuality, it's really how we felt in those moments that permanently marked our minds like a tattoo that can never really be removed without leaving a scar.

Those moments inevitably change who we are. They mold us into the person we are going to become and how we're going to react to similar situations. They either build us up, making us stronger, or tear us down, making us weaker, more vulnerable, more easily hurt. I'm so grateful for the moment in my life that redirected me onto a path I never would have even thought of taking. It not only changed my life; it changed my destiny.

But it was bittersweet.

I was sitting in church with my parents. They had invited me to go with them, knowing I wouldn't have gone otherwise because I didn't want to go alone. They were trying to make sure I didn't feel lonely on this special occasion. I loved them for that. They were doing all they knew how to be there for me during the most difficult, loneliest time of my life. What they didn't realize, though, was that I actually felt more alone in that church room filled with over 300 people than I ever felt when I was home all by myself.

But, honestly, how could they have known that? How could they have possibly understood? They had been married for almost forty years. They were partners in every triumph and every struggle. They were together, every day, without fail, for almost four decades. They had each other to lean on, to depend on, to feel validated by, to sit with, to talk to, to be close to, to laugh with, to cherish and to love.

They had never been apart for more than twelve hours. My dad worked twelve-hour shifts when I was growing up. My mom was always home, waiting to greet him with her beautiful smile and a warm plate of food. Even when he got home at midnight from his 11 a.m. to 11 p.m. shift, she'd be up watching TV until she heard that loud noise our garage door made as it opened, signaling dad's arrival. They'd talk about their day as he ate his meal. Eggs and toast with coffee was his favorite and she knew that. She knew what all of his favorite foods were. They went to bed together and watched TV, holding hands and talking about what they should have for dinner tomorrow. They talked about what items they'd buy on the grocery store run they made together every Saturday. They woke up together every morning and never once missed eating breakfast together.

They had been each other's best friend since before they were married.

They raised my brother and I, demonstrating to us what true love and a devoted partnership really was. They traveled together. Made decisions together. Faced hardships together. Celebrated together. They navigated through life … *together*.

Mom and dad knew one another better than anyone else knew them. They could read each other's thoughts. They were inseparable and everybody knew it. As they aged and eventually both became ill, they took care of one other, each reminding the other to take their medications at the designated times every day. Each one made sure the other was staying hydrated and eating properly, often while rubbing medicated cream on each other when they had aches and pains and going to doctors' appointments together.

They were a united front, and I always knew they'd never, ever depart from the commitment they had made to one another on their wedding day. This is what marriage was to me. A life-long commitment. A God-given right of passage. It's what I had always dreamed of for myself.

Ever since I can remember, I wanted to get married, have children, raise them and grow old together with the same man whom I'd promised myself to until death would "do us part." I wanted "to have and to hold" someone forever, just like my parents had done. I wanted to have a best friend by my side to help me through life's unexpected twists and turns. Someone whom I could lean on when life got hard. Someone to wipe away my tears of joy and also of pain. I assumed I'd have that because that's all I had ever known marriage to be.

I had never seen my parents separated from one other. I had never known marriage to be anything other than a lasting, life-long commitment. As a child, I expected to have the same comfort and security that my mom and dad had. I expected to have my husband by my side to love and cherish me for the rest of my adult life and for me to do the same for him.

Instead, I found myself sitting in church next to my parents as a grown woman in the middle of a divorce on Christmas Eve. My twin toddlers, just four years old at the time, were spending their scheduled parenting time with their dad. As soon as divorce proceedings began, my twins were immediately placed on a court-appointed schedule, dictating which parent they would be able to spend time with on each holiday. We even had specific drop-off and pick-up times to adhere to. Adhering to that schedule was enforceable by law. The law told me when I could be with my own children and when I could not. The legal system by state regulation had invaded my home life and legally separated me from my babies on court-appointed holidays, including this one.

How in the world could this have actually become my reality? To be separated from my babies. To not be able to see them at all during scheduled times with their dad—every other weekend and three weeks of vacation every summer! It was absolute torture for me. My heart ached from the moment I dropped them off until the very moment I saw them again. It was like someone had literally torn a piece of my heart out of my chest and left a big hole there. I felt like I would bleed to death without them. They were my whole heart. Every time they were gone, we were missing valuable time together that we could never, ever get back. I cried myself to sleep the entire time they were gone, *every* time they were gone. Nothing else mattered. I used to lay in their little toddler beds just to feel close to them. It was indescribable.

This particular Christmas Eve was the first one I had experienced with this absolutely horrendous schedule in place. My babies were with my soon-to-be ex-husband and his girlfriend, and I was all alone, even though I was sitting with my parents in a room filled with over 300 people. As I looked around, I saw couples everywhere of all ages. Some young and others old. They seemed to fill the entire church. Married couples, smiling at one another, knowing each other's thoughts, looking into each other's eyes, holding hands and feeling that warm familiarity that a long-term relationship provides.

How I longed to feel loved in that way and to not be alone, re-entering a singlehood that I did not want. To feel the security of a committed relationship. To know that someone would be waiting for me when I got back home, concerned about my well-being and making certain I was safe. To be able to feel like I'm part of something that is so much bigger than myself. To see my future in the eyes of "my person." To smell a familiar fragrance that isn't the one I just put on myself. To be someone's "other half." It seemed that everyone there had someone special by their side on that incredibly special holiday, except me. I felt like I was the only adult there "alone" with my parents.

It's not that my parents weren't special to me. They were so amazing, and I loved being with them. But sitting next to them wasn't the same as having a committed life partner and confidant there by my side. And what about my little babies? They weren't sitting on my lap, to hug, to kiss, to smile at, to hold, to share the joy of our favorite holiday of the year together.

I *loved* being together with my husband and children in church on Christmas Eve. It was miraculous and beautiful. It was always special to me. I'd go shopping at least a month in advance to choose the perfect outfits for them—matching outfits, of course. It's a twin necessity. Oh, how they *loved* to be dressed up for church on Christmas Eve. But now, that was just a memory and no longer a normal part of our lives.

Sitting there in a room filled with all of those happy couples and happy families only reminded me of what I no longer had. I felt broken and empty. I wondered if anyone could see the embarrassment of being all alone, without my husband or children, written all over my face. It was evident I was married because I was still wearing my wedding ring. I didn't want to take it off until I was no longer married. So, on the one holiday of the year that everyone celebrates together as a family, I was without mine.

Christmas is a celebration of the birth of Jesus Christ. I imagined Jesus in the manger, surrounded by His parents and all those who had traveled far and wide to meet Him. How beautiful that must have been for all of them to be together. To me, Christmas is about togetherness. There is an unspoken expectation to be with family on Christmas. But I was without mine. My family –the one I had built and loved with my husband and children—was not together.

This was not my dream. This was a complete nightmare. How could I be in church on Christmas Eve as a mother of two beautiful children alone and going through a divorce?

This wasn't supposed to happen to me. I had my life planned out from the time I was a little girl. My marriage was going to be spectacular. My husband was going to treat me like a princess and make me feel like I was the only person in his world. I was going to love him and nurture him. We were going to be best friends forever (BFFs). I was never going to have to go to bed alone or afraid. He would protect me and honor me all the days of his life. He would defend my honor and make bad days better. We were going to grow older together and take care of each other when we could no longer take care of ourselves.

But now that dream was gone. I was all alone on the most joyous day of the year. Yet, I felt no joy in my heart. It was Christmas Eve, and I didn't even care. It was like a horrible nightmare I hoped that I'd wake up from and everything would be just as I had always imagined it would be.

I was fighting back the tears, trying to "keep it together" for the sake of my parents, who were trying to make me feel better. I didn't want them to know that I was just a few seconds away from bursting out in tears. So, I forced a slight smile as they looked my way. Then, something even worse happened. I could no longer hold back my tears. It was announced that there was a couple amongst the crowd celebrating their 50th wedding anniversary. They were asked to stand up for an applause. Everyone looked around, trying to figure out who they were and where they were sitting. Suddenly, a beautiful couple toward the front of the church very slowly stood. The husband leaned on the pew in front of him for support and his wife used a cane to slowly straighten up. They were well-groomed and perfectly dressed for the holiday in matching colors. The husband had on a black suit jacket with a red tie, and his wife was wearing a simple red dress with a black belt. They both had snow-colored hair sprinkled with a touch of grey and wrinkled skin, a beautiful characteristic of the long life they had lived together. What an honor and blessing it must be to be able to grow old together with your one and only love, just as they had done. They had been each other's "person" for over fifty years.

After they both managed to stand up, he put his arm around her fragile little back. She looked at him and they smiled at one another with the kind of love that was tangible. It was in that very moment that something struck me as hard as a knock on the head. *I would never, ever celebrate a 50th anniversary.* That was something I had *always* assumed I'd have. Now, with a divorce inevitably looming ahead, there was absolutely no way I ever would. This was yet another dream shattered.

I was thirty-two years old, in the middle of a divorce. I was not remotely interested in dating. I hadn't dated in over thirteen years. I wasn't even ready to date, nor would I have wanted to. I was still in love with my family, and I couldn't even think of bringing another person into our lives. My children were my priority. They had to be.

They were unknowingly thrust into a situation they didn't deserve and weren't at all prepared for; nor did they want it. I was not about to allow this divorce to harm them or change them in any way if I could help it. I knew, beyond a shadow of any doubt, that I needed to sacrifice some things for their well-being. They needed stability. Their entire world, as they knew it to be since birth, changed almost overnight without their consent or opinion. Suddenly, they were no longer with mom and dad together ... not ever. They were in different households every weekend, sleeping in different beds. When they were at their dad's, they weren't alone with him. Their dad lived with his girlfriend and her two kids. That was confusing for them. They lost the only real family they'd ever known. They lost the security that a family living together provides. I couldn't change that. But what I could do is make certain that when they were with me, they got *all* of my affection, and my *full* and undivided attention.

So, I knew I wouldn't date anytime in the near future, and I had no intention of marrying again—at least until my children were grown. I didn't want them to have to share me, too. I wanted our home to be a place of solitude and stability for them with consistency and structure. Being married again would rob them of what they needed the most at that time ... *me. All of me.*

I felt like I had failed. I had failed myself, my children, my marriage and my dream. This was something I hadn't been used to. Up until this period of my life, I had worked for what I wanted and had always acquired it. I graduated Magna Cum Laude from high school, earned a full-ride scholarship to Wayne State University, earned a doctorate degree in dental medicine and married my best friend, who also happened to be one of my classmates. We built a new home and collaborated on choosing the floorings, countertops and cabinetry to completely customize it. Together, we started our own business, a dental practice, without partnering with anyone else. We did it all on *our own*. A few years later, I gave birth to twins, a double blessing! Making it even more perfect was the fact that one was a boy, and the other was a girl. My husband and I bought a second home up north to vacation. We had nice cars, boats, snowmobiles and lots of other adult "toys." Everything I had ever aspired to have was mine and then some. My life seemed to be falling right into the exact place I had always wanted it to be.

But sometimes, what we build gets torn down by the destructive nature and evil intent of the one who comes "to kill, steal and destroy" … Satan himself. He can't stand to see us happy. He plans attacks that will tear down the "homes" we build. If we are not properly weaponized for these inevitable attacks, our dreams can be stolen from us, without us even noticing that it's happening. But God is faithful to every one of us … *always*. He can turn what Satan means to destroy us into unexpected destiny.

Before Judas betrayed Jesus, Jesus knew it would happen. He knew it would lead to His crucifixion. Jesus could've stopped it, but He didn't. You see, Satan believed that he was going to stop Jesus from doing what He was sent here to do. Satan knew exactly who Jesus was and he wanted Jesus dead. But Jesus always uses what Satan does to harm us as the very thing to bless us with. Jesus continuously "flips the script" on Satan, and there's absolutely nothing Satan can do about it.

Satan thought if he could arrange for Jesus to be crucified, he could kill, steal and destroy all of the good works Jesus was doing. But what Satan didn't know was that Jesus was planning to "flip the script" on Satan the entire time. Satan had absolutely no idea that Jesus would be resurrected. The only people in the history of the world to have had ever been resurrected up until that point were the people that

Jesus had brought back to life, one of which was Lazarus. So, Satan wrongly assumed that Jesus would be killed and that His destiny would be killed right along with Him. But Satan was wrong.

Satan was also wrong to assume that, when my marriage died, Jesus wouldn't be able to resurrect something better in my life. You see, sometimes we have to hit "rock bottom" in order to find the fight within ourselves to rise up to the top of all that God has for us. We cannot hear Jesus until we stop long enough to listen for His voice. When everything was exactly as I had always dreamed it would be, I didn't need God. I was busy. I didn't make time to stop and listen for Him. I didn't get on my knees and cry out to Him. I didn't surrender myself to Him because I didn't need to. Everything was perfect. I prayed because I was "supposed to." I did what I believed to be good. I donated to charities. I adopted children in Africa to help feed and clothe them. I prayed the same prayers every day, usually right before I went to bed. At times, I fell asleep as I was praying. I told myself that it was ok to do that if I was really tired because God would understand. If I'm being completely honest, I prayed because I thought it would bless me, not because I genuinely wanted to spend time with my Creator. My prayers were memorized, ritualized, and repetitive with some customized requests. They were taught to me by a structured religion. They did not come from my heart, nor from my spirit. I didn't have a personal relationship with Jesus. I didn't even know that I could or should have that with Him. I didn't know Him at all, even though I thought I did. I didn't know His voice. I couldn't feel His presence. I couldn't see His light.

I was living in the dark and didn't even know it. I was not saved, but I was 1000% convinced that I was. I was blinded by Satan and could not discern his deceit through the "veil" that he had placed over my eyes with my own unknowing permission.

Many of us give Satan permission to enter our lives and attack us without even realizing that we're doing it. We watch horror movies about hauntings and satanic rituals, which open doors in our lives for demons to enter. We listen to music about having sex outside the confines of marriage, drinking, taking drugs and rhyming curse words all wrapped up and "hidden" in a clever, catchy tune. We sing along with it, not even knowing that we have just invited demons into our lives and put a curse on ourselves with the words we were just singing.

Even the new age things we do to be healthy and happy draw demons to us, like yoga, even "Christian yoga," burning incense, vaping "calming" anti-anxiety chemicals, reading horoscopes, getting psychic readings "just for fun" or out of a "need to know" if we will get the things we're praying for. These things are demonic.

I didn't know that any of these things brought about spiritual death before Jesus taught me. He spoke to me, and I heard His voice in my spirit. He opened my eyes to the evil things of this world. He had the power to remove the "veil" that I had given Satan permission to place before my eyes. I felt God's presence. He taught me how to forgive and to remove the anger from my heart that kept me enslaved for so long. I stopped feeling sorry for myself. The unbearable pain that had taken residence in my heart was removed as quickly and easily as applying stain remover to a soiled cloth. God showed me that only hurt people hurt others, and that they needed prayer, not persecution. They needed repentance. My soon-to-be ex-husband and his girlfriend, who had not only been our employee for three years, but had also befriended me, invited me to her home and out to lunch, needed prayer. They had lost their way.

Suddenly, I felt compassion rather than anger for those who had betrayed and broken me. My heart was transformed by the sovereign power of almighty God. I knew the "dreams" that had been stolen from me were not God's plans for my life. They were *my* plans. If my "dreams" had been carried out for the rest of my life, they wouldn't have been purpose-filled for the glory of God. My life would've revolved around my own needs, acquisitions and aspirations. That doesn't make me a bad person. But I'm on earth to be the hands and feet of Jesus. I'm here to do His work, His will, and to bless and pray for others. I couldn't possibly do that if I didn't know Him.

Rather than praying and crying for myself, I shifted my focus to those who had hurt me. My prayers became selfless. I asked God to forgive them, I fell to my knees and literally wept for them. I cried out to God to soften their hearts and save their souls. That's when I *knew* I was free!

It was only by fervently seeking God that I found Him. I sought Him in my sadness and in the quiet solitude of prayer time. I would not have been saved or freed from the demonic strongholds that controlled my life if I hadn't been brought to my knees with a pain that had squeezed the joy right out of my life. I cried out to Jesus because I needed Him. I got down on my knees in worship, praise and thanksgiving to Him. It was my passion for Jesus that drew me nearer to Him. The closer I drew to Him, the closer He drew to me. In time, my despair became my surrender, and Jesus healed my heart, strengthened it and softened it all at the same time. Only Jesus can do that with His amazing Grace.

I knew that Jesus never wanted me to feel alone on Christmas Eve or any other time. He didn't want my dreams die. But He did allow it so that I could "see" that nothing on earth is forever. The only thing that is forever is the destination of our soul. I didn't realize that mine was lost. But I thank God every day that now, it is found.

For me, it was in the pivotal moment of watching the older couple rise out of the church pew in gratitude for their 50th wedding anniversary that the trajectory of my own life changed forever. The feelings of failure, defeat and deep sadness that overwhelmed me in that very moment brought me to my knees in surrender to Jesus. This is where *true victory* is found ... on our knees, not on our feet. Jesus did not end my marriage. Satan did. But Jesus "flipped" Satan's "script" by using the death of my marriage to awaken my spirit to life and save my soul.

Isaiah 61:3 says, *"To all who mourn in Israel, he will give a crown of beauty for ashes, a joyous blessing instead of mourning, festive praise instead of despair. In their righteousness, they will be like great oaks that the Lord has planted for his own glory."*

Jesus made beauty from my ashes—the despair, depression and deep sadness. He used something that could've *destroyed* me to actually save me. I will forever be thankful to Him. He continually shows us that we are not alone in any circumstance that becomes an overwhelming mountain and that it is He who is in control.

The first time Jesus gave me a visual sign of His presence and power was when I was a child. It was the first time I realized that the angels I heard and read about were actually real. I was only ten years old, sitting in the backseat of our big, dark blue station wagon. It was a popular car back then. It actually had real wood panels on the outside of the car doors that looked just like the paneling we had inside our house on the walls, another popular fad at that time. I loved that car. It was so roomy. We took it on trips because the trunk space was so big, and it easily stored all of our luggage. My dad was driving. We were going to church. I was on the left side of the backseat, right behind dad. That was my seat. My brother always sat behind my mom on the right side. I was looking out of the window, watching the other cars. As I glanced up toward the sky, I saw a glimmering, gold shape amongst the clouds. I had never actually seen an angel before, but somehow, I knew that's exactly what that was. It had a head, a body and two huge, beautifully majestic wings. It was a floating gold silhouette. It was so beautiful. It's impossible to describe it. I'd never seen anything like it. At the sight of it, an immediate warmth and peace came over me. Then suddenly, as quickly as it had appeared, it was gone. No one else saw it or believed that I had seen it. But that's okay. I don't believe they were supposed to see it because it was just for me.

It was a prophetic declaration that there would be something I would experience in my lifetime during which God would show Himself to me in a way that was hidden to everyone else. I knew in that very moment that I was chosen for something special. I just didn't know what I had been chosen for.

Now, I do. I was chosen to break generational curses and to teach others how to do the same. In my pain, I found purpose by the grace and love of the almighty God. God never allows us to suffer through anything that He hasn't equipped us to navigate. He equips the unequipped. He knows our strengths and weaknesses. He knows what it'll take for us to get on our knees in surrender to Him in order to seek Him fully. If we do not seek God, we will not find Him. If we do not know Him, we will not be with Him for eternity.

Matthew 7:21-23 says, *"Not everyone who calls out to me, 'Lord! Lord!' will enter the Kingdom of Heaven. Only those who actually do the will of my Father in heaven will enter. On judgment day many will say to me, 'Lord! Lord! We prophesied in your name and cast out demons in your name and performed many miracles in your name.' But I will reply, 'I never knew you. Get away from me, you who break God's laws.'"*

Nothing could possibly be more devastating than being separated from Jesus for eternity. If you've lost something that you didn't want to lose—a loved one, a relationship, a marriage, a business, a job, a friendship—know that God is a redeemer, and He will turn your pain into purpose if you let Him. He will not remove the "veil" over your eyes unless you ask Him to remove it. God is a gentleman, and He always restores back to us much more than what Satan has stolen from us.

What I thought I'd lost wasn't a loss after all. It was a lesson and a blessing all wrapped up in one!

RECROWNING & Reflection

1. If you have experienced a pivotal moment in your own life, what realizations or revelations has it awakened you to?

   _____

   _____

   _____

   _____

   _____

2. In what circumstances have you allowed fear, shame, embarrassment or guilt to define you or affect your decisions?

   _____

   _____

   _____

   _____

   _____

3. What lessons have you learned from an unexpected twist in your own life story?

_____

_____

_____

_____

_____

ABOUT THE AUTHOR

Dr. Kathleen Abate

Dr. Kathleen Abate authored her first book, "Dream Big, Live Large," as a way to teach others how to rise up from a fallen place and thrive. Born and raised in Michigan, she enjoys the changing seasons of the Midwest as much as the changing seasons in her life. With a past filled with varying challenges, she has navigated through each season with the direction of God using the gifts, skills and talents He has placed within her.

Dr. Abate has successfully owned and operated Millennium Family Dental in Clinton Township, Michigan since 1999. In 2017, she began a non-profit organization and ministry called Hope's Smile to use the skills she was divinely gifted to bless domestic violence victims, as well as homeless men and women, with dental care they could not otherwise attain.

She is also the proud mother of boy-girl twins who are both currently enrolled in pre-medical programs at Grand Valley State University and aspire to begin medical school next year. Both work part-time as they attend school, Steven as a certified behavioral therapist, and AnnMarie an optometric technician.

Dr. Kathleen Abate aspires to encourage those who have become discouraged by life's twists and turns and to give hope to those who have lost it. She is passionate about helping others to "straighten their crowns" and to know that they are worthy of every good and perfect gift God has for them.

Hope's Smile is a global ministry with goals to reach the ends of the earth with prayer, encouragement and healing. If you'd like to partner with Dr. Abate in blessing the nations, visit www.hopessmile.us to pledge your contribution or to contact Dr. Kathleen Abate directly.

Tainted Lens

LaShana R. Anderson

Someone asked me, "What made you lose your crown?"

Between the ages of four and eight, I was being sexually abused, by not one, not two, but three men who were close to my family. Growing up in the 80s, there was very little talk about molestation, let alone the damaging effects it leaves behind. The only two things I heard about at that time associated with sexual abuse were promiscuity and homosexuality. I was horrified of sex. I also didn't identify with being attracted to the same sex. I couldn't find "me" in promiscuity or homosexuality.

I went through life in a numb place. In a dissociative place. Dissociation was a coping mechanism I used to deal with the trauma of being abused. Being out of touch with myself became a new normal for me. It wasn't until thirty-four years after the abuse started that I realized not only the effects of abuse, but the extent of it. My heavenly Father began to deal with me about intimacy. I am in no way speaking to a sexual relationship between me and my heavenly Father. I do not subscribe to that doctrine.

What He was speaking of was intimacy in regard to closeness. When he brought this to the door of my spirit, I was working and preoccupied with my day-to-day routine. Months went by. To be totally honest, I forgot all about intimacy. Well, there I was, back in my day-to-day routine, with the exception of working outside the home. I was in my prayer room, spending time with the Lord and studying. As I studied my Bible, there it was again: *intimacy*. The title of the study was "Intimacy with God."

My immediate response was, "Okay, God! I hear you." I dug deeper into this intimacy thing. I wanted to know more. I became hungry for more knowledge. I asked the Lord a question: "I pray, study and read my Bible. Why don't I feel close to you?"

His response was, "You have a fear of intimacy."

I know intimacy is a form of closeness, but I didn't know I had a fear of being close. Like most modern-day researchers do, I Googled it. I came across a Wikipedia page for fear of intimacy. I had never been read like that before by someone or something that did not have an audible voice. Wikipedia said, "Childhood sexual abuse patients have an extreme fear of allowing others to see them as they truly are. They have a high fear of being revictimized as a consequence of being trusting and open to someone in authority. Because of their experience, intimacy feels very frightening to most childhood sexual abuse survivors. To feel close to another again is to remember that this position is a dangerous one, one that might lead to being taken advantage of."

I cried like I was at a funeral! My heart was pricked. Not only did being abused sexually affect my natural relationships, but it was also affecting my relationship with my heavenly Father, the most important relationship I have. If my relationship with my Father isn't right, I could just go ahead and throw away all the others. Every month, I participated in a themed fast. This fast included eating one meal a day for the first couple of days. The rest of the fast had other instructions. There I was on this fast. I had already eaten my one meal for that day. Then, something happened.

Dinner was turkey wings, rice and gravy, one of my favorite meals. I was fixing plates for my children when a piece of turkey landed on my finger. I ate it. It was delicious. I even pinched a few more pieces of turkey meat. Then, the best idea came to me. *Girl, just fix a small plate*. For the record, I was not even hungry. I agreed with that idea and followed through. I absolutely delighted in this spectacular meal. I really should've tipped the cook. As soon as I had eaten the last forkful, I heard clear as day, "And you'll even sabotage intimacy."

I ran like Flo-Jo to my prayer room. I dropped to my knees and cried out to the Father to take this away from me. I didn't want to be distant from Him. Thank God He answers prayer. He delivered me from having a fear of intimacy. Although realizing the damage made me sad, I also rejoiced because I was uncovering something that had hid in the corners of my life for far too long. I damaged most of my relationships, especially romantic ones. There are a few men I owe apologies to, and I was so afraid of allowing anyone to see the real me. I feared being *seen*. I was afraid of being vulnerable and expressing my true feelings. I was bound, until my prayers were heard by my heavenly Father.

When I married my ex-husband, all I knew was that I had been sexually abused. I was totally unaware of the extent of the damage that was there, or that there was any damage at all. I wasn't promiscuous or a homosexual, so I thought I had made a clean break. Almost eleven years into the marriage, I discovered I had a fear of intimacy. Now that the wall of the fear of intimacy had been torn down like the walls of Jericho, I was excited to show up in my marriage as this new "free from that" woman.

So, I did what any sincere wife does. I put on my bootstraps and started the work. In the beginning, our marriage was pure fun. We had our own inside jokes, and we spoke frequent movie lines or repeated other lines we'd heard on TV. People loved being around us. We didn't have a perfect marriage; I was happy though. He had his "stuff" and I had mine. One recurring issue in the relationship was words of affirmation. For the one bound with fear of intimacy, affirmation was challenging. I didn't grow up in a home where affirming one another was practiced. We only mentioned the negative and disregarded the positive in our house. After all, we were supposed to do what we were told: get good grades, be responsible and respectable, and maintain your manners. This was my marriage, and I was committed to it until death.

So, I put my big girl panties on and started affirming my husband. I quickly noticed a pattern. I affirmed him by telling him that he's a good father and a good husband. He'd follow up by asking me, "What made you say that?" If you could only see the look on my face.

I always responded with, "Just wanted you to know what I thought."

He'd pry more. "You had to have said that for a reason."

This was his "stuff" showing up. He had some wounds from his childhood that he didn't address. While I was ready to affirm, I wasn't ready to provide a dissertation on why I was affirming him. He made it known that he wasn't getting enough sexual intimacy. As I spoke with other wives, I found that was a common husband complaint. For the record, it was no shortage in that area. That reason was deeply seated also. He also complained that I didn't talk to him much. Our conversations became dry because he always told me what to do. A genuine conversation about my day resulted in responses like, "You should've said this or done that." That's a quick way for me to shut down.

I absolutely hate not being heard. That is something that really gets under my skin. We're both adults. Let me express myself without all the critique. I learned how to navigate in my marriage. Playing nice became something I was good at. We decided I would stay home with the children. His mom was our caregiver, but she became ill and was no longer able to keep the boys. During one of his rants about sex, I jokingly said, "Take me off my job then." The reason I quit my job had nothing to do with sexual expectations. A year after I quit my job, something critical happened.

I wasn't a *person* anymore. I didn't have feelings that mattered. My ideas weren't valuable. I was demeaned by my husband. Suddenly, this new woman who had been delivered from the fear of intimacy, was not able to show up authentically in her marriage. I was looking forward to sharing myself, getting closer to my husband and going on date nights. He was looking forward to more sex, without the willingness to meet my emotional needs. Every single time he touched me while we were in bed, it was to have sex.

I asked, "Can you touch me sometimes without it always leading to sex?"

He said, "No. I can't do that. if I touch you, I'm going to want to have sex."

Triggered is a word we use as a part of our regular vocabulary now, But not so much then. I was definitely triggered and unaware. It felt like I was being molested all over again.

Not long after our eleventh anniversary, we were out running errands. We were both dealing with sensitive family issues with regard to our close external families. He vented all day about it. I shared very little about mine. By the time we were home that evening, I was exhausted. I hit the bed, as if my name was Mike Tyson. He entered our bedroom and asked me a question.

"Why do you think I'm going through all this?"

With no strength in me at all to have any sort of conversation with substance, I looked at him and shrugged my shoulders as if to say, "I don't know." He asked again. I didn't have a different answer. There was this look in his eyes. He had never looked at me like that before. To be honest, I'd never seen him look at anyone like that before.

He left the bedroom and closed the door behind him. Ten seconds later, I heard a loud boom and glass shattering.

I jumped out of bed to find that he'd punched a picture off the wall. The frame had fallen, and the glass from inside the frame broke. This man had never shown any signs of violence before. Something shifted in him that day. And I would be directly impacted by the shift. Remember that this was our eleventh year of marriage. The number eleven means transition or shift. The mysterious beauty of that is you don't know what you're transitioning or shifting into. The transition my marriage shifted into was one that would change my heart and life forever.

After he knocked the picture off the wall, he became more distant. His mom's health had taken a turn for the worse at the time. He was pastoring a church, and he had to leave a job he'd been working at for over twenty-two years to start over. That's enough to make anyone lose themselves. So, I understood. I was careful not to smother him. I didn't want him to feel as if I was disregarding his feelings. But the distance grew wider and wider.

The distance turned into a coldness, almost as if he had turned his heart against me. This man was the nicest of all nice guys. He used to take food to a homeless woman often. But he became so mean to me. It seemed as if, every Sunday, he had an indirect, direct, rebuke for me. It was painfully obvious who he was speaking of. My close friends would leave the sanctuary when his ranting became that intense. I just sat there and stared off into the distance. He stopped being a source of financial support. Outside of the household bills, he offered very little to my pockets. As a stay-at-home mom, this scared me to my core. I totally depended on this man for money. I found myself selling plasma. I can't believe I did that. As a married woman, who expects her husband to provide for her, this shouldn't have happened. Close friends disapproved. But I couldn't stop going. I needed the money.

I interviewed for many jobs, but nothing was coming through. My self-esteem took a blow during the marriage. I did not get married to get a divorce. At the time, the thought of divorce brought a great sense of fear. There's no way I could comprehend something like that wasn't happening. But I was sensing something unsettling. To add insult to injury, he moved out of the house to be able to provide care for his mom. He didn't discuss that decision with me at all. I only saw him a few days a week. He'd be so kind to drop off his laundry, though.

After his mom's death, he had to leave her apartment. Yet, he still didn't come home. This man slept at the church in a folding lounge lawn chair. He finally agreed to go to marriage counseling. Our first session went as any normal intake appointment. When the counselor asked us why we were there, he said, "Well, she was molested as a child."

"Excuse me, sir! We're in marriage counseling because I was molested?"

The therapist quickly informed him of how life is like for sexual assault victims. I appreciated his knowledge and empathy. He explained how walls are built by victims to protect themselves, not to harm others. The therapist started the basic intake questions. Questions about mental health and behavior seemed to spark an alarm for my husband. He was concerned about answering some of those questions because he carried a firearm. He had a license to do so. The therapist assured him one had nothing to do with the other. We continued our session. The therapist stated he would see us the next day to go over his plan of action.

The next morning, I received a call from my husband from work. I'd never heard him sound the way he did. Something was *different* in his voice.

He said, "I have something to tell you."

My heart sank. I knew what he was going to say. I didn't even ask him what it was. I came right out and said, "You're having an affair."

I was in so much denial watching him go through the classic signs of a cheating husband. I thought the man I married would never cheat on me. He confirmed my statement.

"There's something else," he said.

"Is she pregnant?" I asked.

"No."

That was a relief at least. There were so many things that were still unknown. *Who is this person? What are they like?*

He said, "I didn't do what they said I did."

The next couple of minutes were a blur. I don't remember what he said in the moment. I was too devastated for my ears to hear anything else. My heart was completely torn apart. I loved this man. Hearing he was having an affair made me sick to my stomach. I couldn't eat. I'd lost so much weight. I'd always told him if he felt like he ever needed to cheat to just go ahead and divorce me. It didn't make sense to me that he chose this option. The anger that was brewing in me scared me. I punched walls, couches and doors. The funny thing about betrayal is while some moments are okay, the next few moments are not.

We had a picture frame in our bathroom with our marriage license, a picture from our wedding day, and two two-dollar bills to signify one bill amounting to two. In one of my harder moments, I grabbed the picture off the wall and headed to the front door. I was about to send that frame flying out the front door. He grabbed the frame and we wrestled. Somehow, he fell to the ground. I stood over him, yelling at the top of my lungs. I attempted to snatch it out of his hands. He was able to hold on. I'd never been that angry in my entire life. To this day, I'm surprised I didn't cut him.

The woman he had an affair with was now accusing him of raping her at gunpoint. Everything was moving so fast. I could barely catch my breath. We headed back to our second session that evening and dropped this atomic bomb on the therapist. He was even taken back.

"Scratch the plan I had before," he said. Looking at me, he said, "I know you're mad as heck."

I shook my head. I was so numb. First, the affair. Now, legal charges. He had taken some time off work, so he was home with me during the day. I needed some time alone to process this. I'd always said cheating was my deal breaker. Now, here I was, trying to salvage a marriage after my boundaries had been violated and my deal breaker had been broken. The woman he'd been having an affair with worked with him. He eventually got fired since she took the allegations back to work. There were so many gory details with this affair, including sex tapes, emails and audio files.

As a little girl, I loved Whitney Houston. She was so pretty, and her voice was so powerful. I found an audio clip of this woman singing "You Give Good Love" by Whitney Houston. I couldn't listen to that song anymore after that. The pain was real. My husband was eventually arrested. The

U.S. Marshals came to our home to arrest him. My whole world was upside down. We didn't live lives where the U.S. Marshals should be at our door. His bond was a hundred thousand dollars. We had to put our home up as collateral. He was released four days later with a fancy ankle bracelet: a GPS tether.

I'd been to every court date with this man. To this day, being in court gives me anxiety. He received threats from his accuser's child's father. He immediately shut the church down. The woman and her cohorts knew my name. It bothered me that people knew things about me when I was totally unaware of their existence. Feelings of isolation and loneliness gripped me. I had the support of my close friends. However, they had not experienced what I was going through. The last thing I wanted was for my husband to cheat on me. Now we'd been robbed of the opportunity to deal with it in private.

I battled with feelings of not being enough. *What about me is not worth a man being committed to me and only me? What did I do to deserve this? If only I didn't ignore the signs, I wouldn't be hurting this way.* I can't tell you the number of times I played out in my head less painful scenarios. *Why didn't I leave at a certain point? Who are you? Why are you staying?* I had so many questions with no real answers.

I put on my researcher hat again and Googled affairs and affair recovery. I found a support group hosted by a clinical therapist. It was such a blessing. Before I became aware of this affair, I was in such a good place with the Lord. My prayer life was lit. I was fasting and reading the Word of God daily. I couldn't believe this had happened to me. I was so angry with the Lord. I went from being angry with the Lord to feeling like He was angry with me. Many times, when devastation, affairs, death and many other tragic things happen, we are so overwhelmed with what's happening in the moment that we forget all things work together for the good for those who love God.

It began after I arrived at one of my support group meetings. The parking lot was empty. I thought to myself, *A lot of people are running late today.* I grabbed my purse, cup of tea and cookie, and hopped out of my car. As I walked away, I heard something fall. I checked what I had in my hands. Everything was there. The sound of metal hitting the ground continued. I looked down and there was this small, round piece of jewelry. I had worn my favorite necklace to this meeting. I built outfits around that necklace. I loved it. Well, it was falling apart under my coat. I sprang into action, putting my cup of tea on the ground and trying to grab every little piece I could. In my hurry to pick the pieces up, I heard the Lord say, "Let it go."

"Huh? Lord, you remember this is my favorite necklace, right? You want me to let this go?"

The necklace had these chunky balls that, over time, weighed down the string. The clasp was still connected, but the string broke in the middle. The Lord said, "The string would not be able to support the weight of the chunky balls anymore."

The lesson was not to apply more pressure on something that was broken as if it wasn't broken. This word the Lord had spoken to me was the beginning of healing in areas I never imagined. For me, letting go of all the unanswered questions was major. Naturally, I'm an inquisitive person. When I ask questions to the Lord or anyone else, I'm looking for answers. My questions are not rhetorical. Obeying the word the Lord gave, I accepted betrayal. I accepted embarrassment, shame and humiliation. I accepted that I was an overnight single parent after my husband went to prison. I accepted all these things. Acceptance does not equal approval.

I, in no way, put my stamp of approval on anything. But, for me to move on, to let go, I had to first *accept* it. I thought God was punishing me by sending my husband to prison. Every morning, I woke up, flooded with emotion. I begged my heavenly Father to tell me what I'd done wrong. I even repented for things I'd done in the third grade. I never had time to process the affair, criminal charges, public shame, or the way my husband treated me during the time of his affair. The separation is what I needed.

Sometimes, God must remove people for a short time to open our eyes to things we couldn't see. Over time, I got back to my rightful place in God. This whole thing knocked me off my feet and not in a Stevie Wonder kind of way. The Lord showed me my worth and my value. He had not intended for me to be handled that way. The love that I received from my Father resulted in my own personal grow and glow season. I never loved myself. Sexual abuse robbed me of that. Sexual abuse tainted my lens.

Through the lens of self-love, I was able to see that I was willing to settle for less than what I deserved. I deserved to have more than a husband who would cheat on me and land in prison. The love of my heavenly Father and self-love led me to file for a divorce. I took back so many things the devil tried to steal from me. I took back my joy, love, hope and my value. I even took back one of my favorite songs. I can listen to it with no pain today. A smile runs across my face as I sing those lyrics, envisioning my future husband in front of me.

Through it all, I walked away with many valuable lessons. The main lesson was to never, ever betray yourself for love. I betrayed what I needed emotionally, spiritually, financially and mentally to be loved by a man. I overlooked the extent of the love of the One that really mattered: my heavenly Father. The woman I am today is still on a journey of healing. I believe healing is not a destination, but a journey. I'm stronger. I'm more in touch with myself and I'm excited about my future. Never again will I be moved outside of my boundaries. Betraying myself for love is no longer an option. I've been made whole in some areas and I'm continuing to heal. I see a therapist weekly, I read self-help books. I surround myself with awesome people who pray for me, encourage me, and support me.

Today, my crown is intact and in its proper place. It's sitting in the perfect spot. My head is held high—not in pride—but in humility. Whatever I may go through, I will never lose my crown again.

RECROWNING
& Reflection

1. How did your childhood affect your current or past relationships?

   _____

   _____

   _____

   _____

   _____

2. What have you learned from betraying yourself for love?

   _____

   _____

   _____

   _____

   _____

3. How do you take care of yourself through tough times?

   _____

   _____

   _____

   _____

   _____

ABOUT THE AUTHOR

Lashana R. Anderson

If "I don't look like what I've been through" was a person, that person would be LaShana Renee. Rejected in her mother's womb by her biological father, she was sexually abused from the ages of four to eight years old. Thrown into junior parenthood by being forced to help her mother care for her two younger siblings at nine years old, she was bullied on school yards and in a blended family. She was married for almost fifteen years before filing for divorce, mainly due to infidelity. Two absolutely beautiful sons came out of that marriage. But through it all, it didn't make her bitter or jaded.

LaShana has a warm and welcoming personality. She can always see the brighter side of things, and she always has a kind word and a joke or two. LaShana started a journey of healing from sexual abuse and since then has been on a mission to help others along the way, becoming an advocate for sexual abuse victims. She hosted an event during Sexual

Abuse Awareness Month where broken relationships were mended. LaShana is an ordained prophet and became a licensed life and trauma coach to more effectively assist women like herself to heal from deep wounds caused by sexual abuse, rejection and infidelity.

LaShana also started a coaching business, Emerge and See Consulting, LLC, where she focuses on providing a safe place for women to heal. She is such an open book and doesn't mind sharing her story to help others. Her motto is, "They overcame him by the blood of the Lamb and the Word of our testimony." She believes, if we talk about our experiences, we can help stop the bleeding for someone else.

LaShana is a preacher, inner healing and deliverance minister, motivational speaker and a published author. Her writings about her journey of being healed from a fear of intimacy, a failed marriage, how she came out on top and was recrowned can be found in an anthology titled *Recrowning God's Daughters*. Revealing others' stories of lost crowns and redemption, she ministered at women's conferences, and apostolic and prophetic gatherings. For more information, email LaShana at emergeandseeconsulting@gmail.com, or reach her on Instagram at @authenticallylashanarenee and @emergeand_see.

The False Crown

Ronisse P. White

I was sixteen years old, sleeping in the living room, staying the night at her friend's house because all of *our* money went to drugs. Eviction after eviction, we had to move to either a new place of our own or move in with a friend. By this point, I'd attended three different elementary schools, two middle schools, and two high schools. On this particular night, her friend worked the night shift at a hospital. So, she was somewhere in another room by herself—high on crack cocaine.

Out of nowhere, I felt her approach me. She reached inside my shirt where she knew I kept my money.

Is she actually stealing my money from my bra, on my body? I thought, in awe.

At the time, I worked as a hostess at a restaurant, and I made tips each night. So, I always kept a stash in my socks, bra, pockets—anywhere I could hide it from her. But she didn't care. When she needed it, she searched me for it.

But this night ended differently.

Living in the hood, the police rode through the neighborhood with their lights on ridiculously bright to the point they could see inside a home from their vehicles. As the police rode past the house that night, she got the paranoid idea they were looking for her. She thought I called the police on her.

Let's be clear: I was afraid of my mother. My verbally and physically abusive, drug- addicted mother. If I were to call the police, it would've happened a long time ago. At this point, I only had memories of her being an addict, so this was usual behavior. I remember around age seven, I would tell myself, "Things would be so much better without her." I could just live with my grandmother forever.

She believed I had called the police on her and decided she wasn't going back to jail. Furthermore, she decided that neither of us were leaving that house alive. Years of drug usage, verbal and physical abuse led to the ultimate attack on my life.

Up until this point, the only 'weapons' of choice were what a lot of us would call normal or even tough love. Back in the day, it could even be called good parenting followed by the 'spare the rod; spoil the child' Bible Scripture that parents frequently misuse. She used vacuum cleaner devices, textbooks, hangers, hands, feet—whatever was in her immediate reach. I didn't find it normal. Picking out clothes to specifically hide bruises was not my idea of *normal*. Having nail prints on my neck from her tight aggressive grips were not my idea of normal. It also never crossed my mind that she'd progress from a shoe to a deadly weapon. I was just a kid.

On this night though, the tables completely turned.

As the police rode by, she nervously grabbed a knife from the kitchen. She rushed toward me in haste and began poking and taunting me with the knife. I can't recall a single thing she said until she began speaking of how we're both "going to be with Niki"... *in heaven*. Backed into a corner, bleeding through my clothes because the pokes escalated to slices and eventually stabbing, I fought to live! I never fought her back, though. To this day, I can't articulate the level of fear I had in that moment. Fearful and feeling small and helpless, as I always felt, I also felt oddly controlled ... controlled enough that it never crossed my mind to return pain. I just wanted to get away. I didn't desire to hurt her or to help her. I just wanted her to disappear from my world for good. Getting away had been my steadfast stance for as long as I could remember, and I never wavered. Prior to this horrific night, my new belief had already grown to, "I could do so much better for myself without her." At this point, I anticipated adulthood on my own. I was tired of feeling trapped. I knew seventeen was right around the corner, and, in the state of South Carolina, I could emancipate myself without her permission.

What happened next is still a mystery to me. She stopped stabbing and taunting me. She pulled away. It's like she got tired. She went in the room and just laid down on the bed.

I had no idea what was happening or how much time had passed, but the sun was rising. I ran to a neighbor's home to call an older friend. I was unable to go too far as I was bleeding from multiple gashes. I just kept hoping she didn't come after me. I still can't tell you why I didn't call the police myself. Maybe it had been so deeply ingrained in me that if I would have called the police, it could have been worse for me. She always threatened me with *worse*, so I never spoke about the abuse. Maybe deep down I didn't want her to get in trouble. The disconnect and desire to sever ties was so great. My emotions were completely turned off regarding her—almost as if she didn't exist.

This horrific date was July 13, 2000. Ultimately, my friend called the police for me because he couldn't get to me quick enough. The police and ambulance surrounded the neighborhood. But I was so numb from the situation that I didn't remember much of anything after making the call to my friend.

From the hospital, I was released to my dad since I was still a minor. At this point, he had been an absent father as far back as I could remember. As far as I was concerned, the plan was still the same: emancipation. I made my own money, and I was free of drugs and alcohol. I didn't have to answer to anyone. I was finally free of her.

Little did I know that this story was just the beginning. Along with my mom being an abusive, drug-addict mother, she was also a controlling and paranoid mother. I never left the house. I didn't have friends outside of school. I was responsible for being the big sister to my Niki, who had been diagnosed with muscular dystrophy. Unfortunately, at age ten, Niki passed away. While I was anxious and geeked to begin this "life without parental authority," I was clueless to the fact that I knew *nothing*!

I had to live at my dad's house for the first time since he and my mom had legally separated. I had major attitude. I was four when they split, but I can't recall any of our time together. We saw him less than a handful of times in ten years. He lived with another woman and helped raise her children, who weren't his. I felt rejected and abandoned. He didn't know me. I didn't know him. And, to the best of my knowledge at that age, he put forth no effort to correct it. I had no desire to build a relationship with someone who seemingly didn't want anything to do with my sister and me. There was no way I was going from one absent parent to another. We bumped heads all the time. He tried to put a curfew and rules in place for me, but I was not having it. I was already grown! I couldn't wait to be out of his place. I spent one school year with him then did what I knew best – *moved*. I had full confidence that I could do it on my own—and *better*. I moved in with my boyfriend to begin my senior year. I worked and went to school. I thought I was grown and free from toxicity. I quickly became a hot head and a know-it-all.

Just because someone turns eighteen doesn't mean they are grown. My boyfriend and I continued living together after breaking up. Well, this hot head and know-it-all finished high school *pregnant*. We had it out big time because he wanted me to abort. I did not. I left for good.

Hello, single teen-mom.

By this time, it had been almost two years of life without my mother. I was facing motherhood myself and *by myself*. At some point, while I was pregnant, mom and I slowly reconnected. She was consistently sober. She humbled herself and made it her business to be whatever I would allow her to be for me and her first granddaughter.

I was still cold. Still broken. Still extremely hard on the outside. Still lost. Still a fearful, abandoned little girl inside. I gave birth two days before my nineteenth birthday. But something still told me, "You're still going to be so much better than she ever was. You've got this."

Along the way to what I thought was freedom, I laid down my crown. I used her hurt. I lashed out. I treated her like she owed me and deserved whatever I had to give. I knew I needed her. But at this point, the false crown of entitlement was much shinier. It fit much better. It felt deserving.

I intentionally share the heaviest part of this story because some believe a parent deserves whatever they get. In some way, they've earned the damaging and broken behavior that is dished out by their hurting adult children. Sometimes, the hurt and dark experiences are so overwhelming, so offensive and so unfair that the thought of stepping outside of it to seek understanding can also feel unfair. It can seem like, "All I just had to endure and now you want *me* to try and understand?"

What about my deprived childhood? What about the lack and abuse I suffered involuntarily? What about me having to endure these times without my baby sister? What about this unending feeling of unworthiness? What about this new little human I'm responsible for? I didn't see a loving parent in my household. How do I lead my kid when I don't even know how to lead myself? Matter of fact, *who am I?* In those times I lashed out, I was led by my feelings rather than the Spirit. And it further kept me bound. Thankfully, I've grown to realize that our feelings are untrustworthy. Faith and following Christ does not allow for feelings to take lead. Hebrews 11 reminds us of that. Proverbs 3:13 also instructs us to obtain understanding.

Seeking to understand someone else's plight doesn't always come easily, but the Father never advised it would be easy. It could be especially difficult when you're on the receiving end of abuse from a parent. We expect parents to protect and lead, at bare minimum. That was not my case for either parent. I did nothing to cause it, and I couldn't do a thing to fix it. However, once I became of a responsible adult age, I realized that in everything I was then experiencing, my mother was in a battle of her own that had nothing to do with me.

My dad was in a battle of his own.

Mom could not love, parent or raise me beyond what she knew. Those adult years of rebellion, entitlement, disregard and flat-out disrespect were not because I was unaware. It was because, in my mind and in my feelings, it felt right. I was cold and I felt justified.

From mom's vantage point, she endured a battle with the disease of drugs and alcohol off and on for twenty years. She internally faced challenges of feeling unloved, abandoned, rejected, outcast and unworthy. They were very real for her and now reflected in me.

Does gaining understanding dismiss the abuse and neglect of my childhood? No. Does it condone her actions of attempting to take my life? Of course not. I do not for any reason condone abuse. However, in laying down my crown and wearing the "I could do so much better for myself" crown of judgement and pride, I carried the cycle on.

Broken.

I began parenting from the same book, just a different chapter. My wounds of unresolved trauma needed exposure in order for me to recognize how relatable my life was becoming to the life I was running from. I didn't need to drink or do drugs to keep the broken cycle going.

I had to starve my ego. It took me over eight years to receive the revelation of forgiveness in this area. It took me being a struggling single mother to realize I'm literally living what I could not wait to get away from. Similar to drinking and doing drugs, I found validation at my place of work. I found comfort in being in long-term relationships. These were my drug of choice. Same book, just a different chapter.

If any of this resonates with you, you know that it's only a matter of time before my daughter, a new generation, will experience some level of the same broken, inferior thoughts. This generational brokenness had an expiration date and healing needed to begin.

One night, I found myself driving and crying uncontrollably. I parked in a city park a few miles from my home, looked over at a borrowed Bible in the car, and opened it. I landed on Romans 12. I read it over and over, particularly verse two. It lit my heart and gave me hope. I fell in love with the entire chapter that night. I couldn't remember the last time I'd intentionally picked up a Bible to read it. In that very moment, God was renewing my mind. The beginning of transformation was taking place. I could actually feel God shifting and working within me.

I could not progress in anything else with the mindset I had previously. I couldn't be the daughter my mom still needed me to be. I couldn't even properly love and lead my daughter until this revelation was received and I took steps to a renewed lifestyle. It required me to reevaluate my circle. Think of a time your friendship or relationship palate began to change. Was it a pretty smooth process or was it excruciating like mine? I didn't want to let go of some of the things that were feeding this now dead lifestyle. One of the relationships I held a tight grip on fed my entitlement. When I needed to vent about my mother, I knew exactly who to call. That person validated how I was feeling. They knew the right things to say to encourage my thought process. On the other hand, I was connecting with people who countered my negative thought processes. This is the power of community. This helped promote change. Ecclesiastes 4:9-10 reminds us of the importance of a strong village. I developed godly accountability and hadn't even caught on to it. I could tell transformation was happening, though. Eventually, I was no longer someone those old friends wanted to spend time with.

Now, I'm not going to sugar coat it. It can start out feeling a little isolating. In a sense, I went from rocking a crown made of this world, shaped in bitterness and pride, having big *irresponsible* fun to having my Father place His crown back upon my head. One could relate this time of transition like going from a long-time toxic team to one of growth, unity, and high integrity. In that time, you can go from being a star player on the toxic team to being a new kid on the block of a team with an unfamiliar play book. It can be quite uncertain. But this time it's a better, foundationally solid, team- with greater pay. But the in-between is as temporary as you allow it! Being God's daughter and being intentional about building a relationship with Him reminds me that I can walk in peace during every storm. I can pull on His strength when things seem unbearable. I can trust that my joy is renewed daily. In this process, I was invited to a church. I didn't go right away. But when I finally did, I never looked back.

For the first time in my adult life, I joined The Faith Center in Tucker, Georgia at age twenty-eight. Being under anointed leadership, planted in a Bible-based church that radiates the love of Christ is most certainly a contributor to learning how to love myself. I'm spiritually grounded enough to continually hear and understand how to love His people.

I proudly wear my crown as I am a daughter of the Most High God. It's a daily decision to look beyond the flaws and hurtful decisions of others. It's a daily and rewarding decision to choose to seek understanding. It's a daily decision to choose to love and choose to forgive. *Daily*. This is the inner work that's necessary to look back at mom and dad through a new lens. You may not forget; however, as Christians - followers of Christ, I encourage you to take just one step forward. Even if that step doesn't look the same as anyone else's- just go for it.

One of the more important takeaways in reconciling with my parents was that, with each approach, I had to learn not to expect them to be on my level of readiness. Sometimes parents, for many reasons, haven't seen it from your perspective. They may not believe a discussion or reconciliation is necessary. They may not view your hurt as a big deal. Sometimes they may not be ready to face or uncover a situation from however many years ago. I totally get it. Let God be God for them like He is for you.

I had a conversation with my dad regarding something he said that I believed was pretty insensitive. It stayed with me for a long time. During a random conversation, I decided to ask him what he meant by it. He felt the same way as he had before. He didn't realize it hurt me, though. He apologized that my feelings were impacted, but he never changed or adjusted his stance on it. I had a responsibility to respect how he felt and to keep the space safe so we could continue to connect and have open dialogue.

On the other hand, my mom and I have conversations quite often where I may be a little more firm than she is on a matter. She jokingly says I get that from my dad; she's right. She's my best friend but we certainly had to grow to get here. I respect the fact that we think differently and have varying perspectives. This further opens the lines of communication. This is the goal. This is where we want to be; quickly forgiving and beautifully flourishing.

RECROWNING & Reflection

1. Healing in every area of your life is your covenant. What does this statement mean to you?

   _____

   _____

   _____

   _____

   _____

2. If you don't have the relationship you desire with your parent(s), what would it look like if you did?

   _____

   _____

   _____

   _____

   _____

3. Ask your parent or parents about a time when they felt abandoned and rejected. Make it a light, casual conversation. Listen and receive without judgement or feedback, just with the intent of hearing and understanding from their perspective and emotional capacity at the time. What was their response?

4. Is there an area of your life negatively impacted by a parent, but you haven't visited it in a while? What aspect of your present or future would look different if that area were healed?

ABOUT THE AUTHOR

Ronisse P. White

𝓡onisse White is a worshipper of Christ Jesus, licensed minister, certified life coach, youth advocate, author, and a distinguished visionary who is dedicated to empowering women to break through inferior thinking in the way of God's truth to unlock their divine destiny. She is passionate about helping others become the very best version of themselves. Her areas of keynote teaching include life purpose, conflict solutions, goal success, and reconciliation of the parent adult/child family dynamic.

Having experienced feelings of unworthiness brought upon by a childhood of neglect and abuse, she learned to use adversity as a steppingstone for herself through the help of Christ. She has dedicated intentional time to helping women, families and children create a life aligned with the Word of God. Ronisse is known for the vibrant, powerful, and passionate manner in which she encourages and empowers God's people. She is godly proud to be a resource and aid in the direction of healing for women across the globe.

She is a true woman of God, devoted to the purpose in which God has predestined for her. Ronisse is a proud food connoisseur and is known for conducting her coaching and empowerment sessions around the comforts of a great meal. She is married with one young adult daughter and is extremely proud of them both. For more information, visit www.lnk.bio/Ronisse.

Crowned Identity

Nicho Charisse

I'll do my best to describe what caused me to lose my crown and what the process of healing looks like for me. I learned too many lessons to count. For years, I didn't even know I had such a priceless, intangible item. I didn't know I was blessed with it before I was created in my mother's womb. It's hard to believe you have such a possession when most of your life has been surrounded by selfishness, molestation, bullying, and the varying recipes for low self-esteem. I wish I was a little girl who was raised as a princess and groomed to become a woman who becomes a queen in my own castle with a king. Life didn't happen that way, but I do wear my crown proudly.

I Don't Think She Was Ready

Before I deep dive into this, let me start by saying that I love my mother. I did not *like* her sometimes, but I love her. Many relatives told me that my mom was scared to hold me when I was born. As a matter of fact, she didn't hold me for a while. I'm sure it's hard for people to believe that a woman would not want to hold her baby after childbirth. However, when my daughter was born, she did the same to her. Therefore, my mom and I never bonded the way I thought that we should have. My mom is, in my opinion, a very beautiful, yet very vain, selfish woman. Men flocked to my mom. They always wanted to be around her. She took me in the bars with her because I was "cute" enough for her to get free drinks and a new boyfriend. I was able to get free ginger ale and quarters to play Pac-Man, so I didn't completely complain.

Most of my childhood, we lived in a one-bedroom apartment. This meant less room and less closet space. I had to sacrifice my belongings in order to keep her clothes intact. Because of limited drawers and closet space, my clothes were always stuffed in small areas. Heaven forbid that my clothes were in the closet and touched or wrinkled her clothes. She always made sure she had expensive shoes and other accessories. If I was in bed sleep, and she had a male companion come to the apartment, she woke me up and made me sleep on the couch. My mom always came into the living room to see if I was sleep. I pretended like I was most times. That was her queue that it was okay for her to have sex.

Our local radio station, WAMO, played slow songs at night. For years, I disliked the song *Sweet Baby* by George Duke. When it came to men, I don't think my mom had a type, as long as they took care of her. One of the men she dated looked like an extreme dark Rasputin. I watched a man physically abuse my mother. He bought her many things. But if he didn't get his way, he would destroy it all and raise his hands to her. I pulled a knife on him and vowed to never let a man do that to me.

During that time, I was a latchkey kid. If my mom worked or was out on a date, I knew the rules:

1. Don't answer the door for nobody.
2. If anyone calls, tell them she is busy or sleep. Take a message.
3. Don't touch the stove.

I spent most of my time watching television and talking to my paternal grandmother on the phone. I didn't know it at the time, but my grandmother called my dad and told him every time I called. When I left my mother's home and moved in with my grandmother, my mom didn't hesitate to sign over guardianship. The day we were scheduled to go to court, my mother got there early so she could sign the paperwork without seeing me. That same week, my mother sued my father for child support.

To this day, she still wants someone to take care of her. She is still extremely materialistic. As I have grown, I don't really believe she was ready to be a mother. She was overwhelmed. She tried her best with the tools she had in her wheelhouse. I don't even believe my mother understands the crown she possesses. She watches me today, and she is amazed at the way I live. I tried to raise my kids differently. I tried to deal with all relationships differently than she has, including her relationship with me.

I was molested by three different men. Two of them were my mother's boyfriends. The other man was my grandfather. The first boyfriend was a cop. He was a man who was supposed to serve and protect me. Instead, he was teaching me how to kiss at the age of five years old. There was a children's clothing store in downtown Pittsburgh called Lloyds. Around Eastertime, he bought me a dress. The top part of it was red with white polka dots, and the bottom was white. It came with a blue cloak. The cloak reminded me of Juliet Mills when she played in *The Nanny and the Professor*. After he took me to get that dress, he had me put it on with white tights and white Mary Jane shoes. That was the first time he kissed me— tongue and all. I don't remember him doing anything else. But every time he watched me while my mom was out of the house, he kissed me … and I kissed him back.

My maternal grandfather was about my complexion, but he was not a fan of dark-skinned blacks. I had heard the stories that my grandfather always wanted my uncle to date extremely light-skinned or Caucasian women. My mother was no different. He wanted her to be with lightly complexed or Caucasian men. He had my uncle go to my mom's prom and bring her home because he didn't like my mom's date.

My grandfather spent his time and money on my light-skinned cousins, but not me. Even when my mom and I lived with him, he didn't want to deal with me—except when he molested me. When he watched me, he made me sleep in the bed with him and he made me perform oral sex on him. He was a large man. There I was, moving a grown man's belly to pleasure his penis or suck on his man boobs, as if they had milk and I needed nourishment.

My mom was also seeing another man when I was in the fifth grade. She worked mostly during the daytime, so she was gone early in the morning. He waited a while to make sure she was gone. Then, he'd lie beside me, naked. He taught me how to pleasure his penis—first with my hands, then my mouth. After a while, he tried to penetrate me.

The joke about men who say, "Just let me put in the tip" is no joke at all. Eventually, he became tired of this happening on the couch. He made me come into the bedroom. The final straw for me was when he wanted me to perform oral sex on him. This time, he placed his penis in my mouth and told me not to move. Suddenly, he urinated in my mouth and wanted me to swallow it. I couldn't. I jumped out of the bed and ran into the bathroom. I threw up. He never touched me again. I'm not sure why he and my mother finally broke up, but I was glad he was gone. Especially since, during this time, I was still dealing with my grandfather. The molestation only ended when I ran away from home and moved in with my paternal grandmother. But there were other things happening during this time.

Courage in a Bottle and in Hand

There's an old saying that goes: "You don't really know someone until you move in with them." I didn't know how heavy of a drinker my paternal grandmother and uncle were until I ran away from home. When I arrived at my grandmother's house, she wasn't there. I knew that my aunt and uncle lived across the street from her, so I went there. My aunt answered the door. However, she talked to me with her teeth clinched. I didn't know at the time that her mouth was wired shut because my uncle had beat her up and broke her jaw. My grandmother was out of town at the time. I stayed with my aunt and uncle overnight, but I returned home to my mom the next day.

Once my grandmother was home, I began the transition to move in with her. As the years went by, I toggled between my grandmother's and my mom's house. Having my own room at my grandmother's was nice, but I ran to my mom's when she became extremely drunk. My grandmother threw things at me when she couldn't get her way with me. One time, she threw a flashlight at me. I caught it, but reflex made me throw it back at her. The flashlight broke in half on her shin. She has pulled a knife and a gun on me a few times. I have watched my uncle beat up my aunt too many times to count.

When she was seven months pregnant with their third child, he came home drunk and started a fight with her. I got in between them to protect her. He picked me up and slammed me against their wall unit. It gave her enough time to run out of the house and get to her mom's. My aunt finally became fed up and stabbed him in the chest about an inch away from his heart. They finally divorced. My uncle finally went to jail. I left my grandmother's house after high school graduation. To this day, I do not smoke nor drink.

From fourth grade until my freshman year of high school, I was bullied. Every day during the school year, there was a chance I was going to get into a fight. I may have been fighting one person. Sometimes, I was fighting up to four people. But it happened. Some of my teachers would let me leave school early. If I couldn't leave home to either get into the building early or take another path, I was sure to get into a fight. I have been jumped on by students on school buses and in locker rooms. One time, I was sitting in art class. A group of girls convinced the largest girl in the class to walk over and punch me in the face. She knocked me out of my chair onto the floor. My eighth-grade year, a girl told the entire school that she was going to beat me up after school. The school buses were parked in the back of the school. I walked outside and was jumped by multiple people. A guy held my arms behind my back so another girl could come after me. When she came close, I kicked her in the stomach—not knowing she was pregnant. My social studies teacher told the principal that if all involved were not suspended, she was going to protest.

We all had to go to juvenile court. My freshman year of high school, a boy started picking on me. He was wearing a cast on his leg, but that didn't stop him from fighting me. Our biology teacher attempted to break up the fight and ended up on the ground with spine damage. I had to go to juvenile court again, but the boy was sent to a juvenile detention center because he had previous altercations with students and teachers at another school. Most of the bullying and teasing was because of my name. I was teased mostly because I have a gap in my tooth and because my grandmother and I were on welfare. I was also teased because of my complexion.

Apparently, Love Has Color

My maternal grandfather was not the only one who had a problem with the color of my skin. I had been friends with a young lady since the eighth grade. She had a brother who I thought was very good looking, but I never thought about telling him that. My senior year, we began dating. I wasn't allowed to have company at my mom's house, but I would sneak people over there sometimes any way. One day, his sister called me. He asked her to break up with me because I was too dark. Never in my wildest dreams did I imagine a boy breaking up with me because of my complexion. A few months later, he murdered his girlfriend with a Samurai sword through her heart; she was Caucasian. He got life without parole. In 2012, he asked his sister to reach out to me because he wanted me to testify on his behalf about his character so he could be released. I did not.

There was a time in my life when I always wore baseball caps. My favorite cap had a logo of a fancy cat with the brand name Baby Phat written on the front. I went to the beauty supply store and purchased a new one every time there was a new color, including black, red, white, dark blue, light blue and khaki brown. I had been pulled over a few times, but always at night. A couple of times, I knew it was my fault. I hadn't been very responsible with my finances. My car insurance lapsed often and, of course, when the police ran my plates, it showed them that I had expired insurance. Somehow, I found a good excuse, and they always let me go. It threw me off when the police officer shined his flashlight on me. He always had a surprise look on his face. I never knew what the surprise look was about until the last time I was pulled over.

My mom and kids were in the car. It was a sunny afternoon as we drove down Frankstown Road toward Homewood. I saw the police cruiser behind me. Suddenly, he turned on his lights and sirens. My insurance was up to date. My car had been inspected, and my registration was up to date. I pulled over and the cruiser parked close to me. He didn't rush to get out. I looked in my rear-view mirror and saw him on his radio. He finally got out the car. But instead of coming toward me, he went to the passenger side. He saw my kids, then my mom. He looked at me with the same surprised look as the previous cops before speaking.

"I'm sorry! I thought you were a guy. There was a shooting nearby and the description was a black male wearing a red baseball hat."

I was wearing my red Baby Phat cap. All this time, I was being racially profiled because I look like a male while wearing a hat.

My first marriage was to a man who was light-skinned, and he had what some would consider "pretty hair". He is of Native American decent. He has a deep voice, freckles, and jet-black, curly hair. When he let his hair and beard grow long, my kids' classmates called him Osama Bin Laden. My mother-in-law and sister-in-law didn't like me because, not only was I a single mother who lived in low-income housing, but I was dark. When our son was born, the neighbor and my mother-in-law talked about how glad they were my son turned out to be light-skinned. I haven't seen my son since 2010. He is now twenty-five years old, and he tells everyone that he hates me. In his eyes, he does not have a mom or sister.

The More You Grow, the More You Know

"They can't hurt me anymore" is what I always say when I talk about the things that have happened to me. I know I am not the only one who has been through these things, and I don't want anyone to feel like they are alone. I have lost my crown, laid it down, damaged it, thrown it up against the wall, ran over it with my car, thrown it into the ocean, lake, rivers and ponds—all while not knowing *I even had a crown*. I had to ask myself again, "When did someone tell me that I was a princess, a queen, and a woman who possessed a crown? When did someone tell me I was beautiful inside or outside?" I was not born or raised in the church. I went to church off and on throughout my life, but never consistently. When I lived with my father, I went to a Methodist church with him and a Catholic church with my stepmother. I have attended Baptist and non-denominal churches, as well. I decided to continue my journey in my faith, and to learn and understand the Bible. I better understood my relationship with God and better understood myself. I better understood who I am. I understood the things I have gone through. I have cried a lot. I have had to walk away from people to find *me*. I thank God for His grace and allowing me opportunities that too many people take for granted.

Your Crown is Your Superpower

Ororo Munroe was born to a tribal princess of Kenya and an African American photojournalist father. She was raised in Harlem, New York City and Cairo, Egypt. She was made an orphan after her parents were killed during an Arab–Israeli conflict. A master thief trained Orono to become a pick pocketer to survive. She soon discovered that she had powers from a professor who took her under his wing. Her ability to manipulate the weather and fly has made her one of the most powerful mutants of her time. She was taught how to use and control her powers while dealing with being claustrophobic. Ororo is also known as Storm from X-Men. Jennifer Pierce started freaking out when she started developing powers, especially once she and her family soon found out her powers have been growing at an unusually fast pace. She quickly mastered her powers of superhuman strength and durability. Jennifer struggled to understand how her lightning-based powers worked, especially once she learned that, unlike her father, who was essentially a living battery, Jennifer was a generator whose cells were constantly creating large amounts of energy. Jennifer is also known as Lightning, the youngest daughter of Black Lightning. Though they both are fictional characters, they were clueless about their powers. Once they were introduced to them, they had the choice to use their powers for good or bad. Just like with superpowers, crowns come with responsibility.

November 2, 2022, I will celebrate my 50th birthday with a better understanding of who I am as a woman and a child of God. I am thankful for the storms, the darkness, the good, the bad and the ugly. I am glad that, despite my journey, I still walk with an open mind and a heart filled with love and understanding. Looking back on what I have gone through lets me know that my story can possibly help someone else.

I'm still here. This is my truth. These are my heartbreaks. This is my testimony.

RECRONING & Reflection

1. Have you ever considered the responsibility of being blessed with a crown from the Most High?

   _____

   _____

   _____

   _____

   _____

2. When have you felt like your crown was a heavy burden?

   _____

   _____

   _____

   _____

   _____

3. What have you done that made you feel undeserving of your crown?

   _____

   _____

   _____

   _____

   _____

4. When have you helped another sister / friend understand and nurture her powers?

   _____

   _____

   _____

   _____

ABOUT THE AUTHOR

Nicho Charisse

For Nicho Charisse, writing was not an essential part of her life. It was a way to keep her insanity while having to sit in meetings. There, she created stories and used the people in the room as characters. Her first published piece, "What's Next?", was inspired by a rip in a friend's chair that she repaired. It was written months prior to being introduced to an anthology called *Reflections on Purpose* under Expected End Entertainment Publishing. Thanks to the encouragement of C. Nathaniel Brown, she went on to write: "Dear D" under *Dear Depression*; "The Little Things of Human Nature" under *In the Morning*; and "The Ugly Cries" and "You Will Hit Rock Bottom" under *I Thought You Should Know*. In addition, she has "Butta and Skin" and "The Attic" in the anthology *Mr. and Mrs. Toxic 3: The D'Angelo Theory* under the pen name Demetria Amir Ellis. They are published under Emotional Fiction Publishing created by Nikki Flowers.

Nicho is part of a panel on YouTube and a podcast called *Voice 4 the Voiceless: Sexual Abuse Survivors*. Her goal is to be a voice for those who are afraid to tell their story but want to be heard. She is also in the process of writing a book and hopes to have other victims of abuse included. She hopes to be able to help others through their healing process and possibly create a support group.

Nicho is working on a novella and other projects under Bolden Alter Ego (BAE) in hopes to one day have them discovered by the likes of Tyler Perry, Shonda Rhimes, Jordan Peele and Isa Rae. Nicho does not limit herself to one genre for she feels, if you limit yourself, you have self-doubt. You can follow Nicho Charisse on IG @Demetria_Amir_Ellis or email boldenalterego72@gmail.com.

The Lost & Crown

Siobhan R. Flynn

Lack of self-identity caused me to lose my crown. At a young age, the men in my life created negative environments around me. I actually remember when I laid my crown down. I was in my late teenage years. It took many unwanted situations to occur before I even realized the significance of my crown. Not only did I lose my crown, but it went through damage, as well. After several years, I continually kept the crown on my head.

At the age of six, it began with the men in my life speaking hurtful things to me and doing hurtful things to me. The male figures in my presence lacked the ability to pour into my life. Girls need to see their fathers in a positive light to see a healthy example of a man. By nature, girls need a positive male example to guide her in the right direction in terms of how a man should treat her. As far back as I can remember, the men in my life have always spoken down to me. This included my grandfather, uncles and male friends of my stepfather.

At the age of six, I was in the back seat of my stepfather's car. It was early in the morning, long before the sun came up. They woke me up to ride along while he took my mother to work. My mother was a nurse and she worked very early shifts. So, my stepfather dropped her off at work and babysat me and my newborn sister. There I was, still in my pajamas, with my favorite blanket in the middle rear seat of the car. While stopped at the red light, I could hear voices outside of the car.

My stepfather saw someone he knew in need of a ride. Once the light turned green, he pulled into the parking area of the Coney Island and opened the passenger door. He let the man into our car. As we drove off, the cracked passenger window pushed the strong aroma of vomit to the backseat. As my stepfather drove, this man turned around and looked at me with the smell of alcohol on his breath. The old man asked my stepfather a question. Little did I know the next response from this old man would snatch the very innocence from my soul.

"Who the heck is she?" the man asked.

"You know who that is. It's your granddaughter, Bonnie. Bonnie, tell your grandfather good morning," my stepfather said.

"She is no grandchild of mine!"

"Good morning, granddaddy," I said.

The old man turned around and, instead of replying with, "Good morning," he called me vulgar names in a threatening tone of voice.

"Shut up talking, you little female dog! You ain't nothing but a whore, and you will never be nothing in life!"

"Why would you say that to her? Stop it right now!" my stepfather yelled.

"Daddy! I want to get out," I cried.

"It is going to be okay. He didn't mean those things. He is drunk, and we have to take him home," my stepfather said.

I was in the backseat crying my eyes out. I could literally feel something leave my heart. I was too young at the moment to understand how serious this moment was in altering the foundation of who I would become. I was too young to know what drunk really meant. One thing was for certain: this definitely broke something deep within me. At the age of nine, my stepfather invited Uncle Travis and his friend Percy over to the house to work on their cars while mom was at work.

Percy was a middle-aged man who seemed to be passive aggressive. One summer morning, my stepfather and Uncle

Travis left me in the house for a few minutes while they left Percy in the house to go to the bathroom. Uncle Travis and my stepfather went to the garage to start repairs to a car. Percy came out of the bathroom and had a seat on the couch next to me.

"Come here, girl," he said. "Come sit down and talk to me."

He was tapping his right hand on his right thigh. I grabbed my toy and went to sit on his lap. He touched my ponytails and asked me questions. I could smell the aroma of alcohol on his breath. He then placed his hand on my thigh and moved his hand under my shorts, past my panties. I felt his rough finger moving around inside of me. My heart raced and I felt sick to my stomach for a few minutes. Percy touched me in a place that I knew was not right. I was confused at how this happened so fast. I could not understand it. These five minutes changed my life forever!

I told him to stop, and I started getting off his lap. I heard my stepfather and uncle getting closer, which prompted him to leave me alone. Moving forward, every time Percy came over, he hit me on my rear end and called me "ugly girl" or other vulgar names when my parents were not around. I grew terrified of this man! I was in fear of sharing this with my parents. They argued many nights. I just wanted a few nights of peace in the house, with no chaos. I didn't want to risk losing my mother and stepfather to death or incarceration.

Therefore, I carried this terrorizing secret into my adulthood. Moving forward, I was easily persuaded by compliments and attention from boys and men. As time went on, I hardly saw Percy or my grandfather. By the start of high school, my stepfather was tragically killed. Even though I was now a teenager, those negative words and actions stuck to my heart like glue. I allowed those words to continually shape and mold me into the young lady I was becoming.

At the age of seventeen, I discovered my crown. I knew that only queens wore crowns. Based on the labels placed on me, I clearly did not believe I could be royalty. I did not know the importance of my crown, but I knew it was there. I didn't even know what to do with a crown. I learned nuggets of etiquette along the way during childhood through my mom even though my mother spent most of her childhood in foster care.

I think my mother knew she had a crown, but she could not articulate the fullness of her crown due to the lack of examples in her life. Nevertheless, she was a beautiful woman, inside and out. She taught me the most important component that would help me through life. At the age of fourteen, she introduced me and my two sisters to God and a consistent prayer life; I thank her for the introduction. At the age of seventeen, I took my crown off, placed it on the shelf, and did not look back. During my senior year of high school, I met an older man while working my after-school job.

I was only seventeen, and he was twenty-eight years old. We were together daily. Sometimes, he would even pick me up from school. We were sexually involved almost daily. I was sassy and proud to be dating an older man. I felt sophisticated and sufficient when we were together. A few days before graduation, this man was exposed for being *a cheater to his wife and two children.* My mother had done her investigation on him and told him to never call me again or else, he would go to jail. During this time, I was unaware of his background. I never considered he could be lying. I felt insufficient and embarrassed.

By the age of nineteen, I was expecting my first child and I was married after six months into the relationship. After the wedding, he treated me like a possession. There was always vulgar name calling and physical abuse. My mind and body were not my own. Even though I worked a full-time job, he was in control of the finances. I turned my entire paycheck over to him biweekly.

He chose the clothes that I wore and the places I went. One evening, I came home late from work. I felt the tension rise in our conversation about me arriving late. I grabbed my son's diaper bag, my purse and my keys to make a subtle run for the front door to the car. As I ran to the car with our one-year-old son in my arms, I caught a forceful fist to the eye, which caused me to fall straight to the ground with the baby still in my arms. I quickly protected the baby by covering him while I curled into a fetal position.

He continued to kick my weak body while I remained huddled with the baby in the middle of the dark street pavement. As he ran into the house, I managed to get into the driver's seat of the car with my son on my lap. I drove to the nearest police station, speeding in panic and awe, with no car seat or seat belts. I promised God that if He got me out of this situation, I would have a relationship with Him for the rest of my life. When we arrived at the hospital, the emergency room staff told me that if my son had injuries, he had to go into temporary foster care. Thankfully, my baby had no injuries, not even a bruise or scratch.

I left the hospital with a black eye, bruised ribs and two fractured fingers from blocking the punch. For two weeks, I was in the house. I didn't want to come out into the world. I was sensitive to light, ashamed and embarrassed. I thought to myself, *Why me? I don't deserve this, but I love him. I've been talked to like this my whole life so this must be normal, right?* My life is far more important than receiving an apology gift to make up for the suffering inflicted on me. I acknowledged the crown sitting on the shelf, but never considered putting it back on. I still was unable to recognize my self-worth. I knew I deserved better. I knew God didn't intend for me to live my life in fear, unhappy, broken and bruised. I believed there was beauty on the other side of all the negativity. Therefore, I chose to walk away from the title of a battered wife.

At the age of twenty-two, I met an older man who became my best friend. This man was twenty years older than me. He introduced me to more positive things in life. I had been used to men coming into my life and ripping me apart, instead of adding to me. He was the first man to come into my life who acknowledged and enlightened me on my own crown. The first few dates we had were amazing.

He told me that I was a queen and men are kings. He explained that men have crowns, and he started asking about my crown. The first thing we did together was reach for my crown. Then, he sat me down to explain how a queen should think and act. We went to elegant dinners and jazz concerts. He introduced me to chivalry. He opened doors for me, sent me flowers just because, and even pulled my chair out at restaurants. His voice was always calm, and we even prayed together. Our conversations were driven by purpose and affirmations.

I was convinced he was sent from heaven to introduce me to a better lifestyle and to show me the significance of my crown. Learning the significance of my crown was only the start of my new journey. Even though I was aware, I continually put the crown on the shelf in the form of settling. I was moving in a way that felt familiar, but it was not a good situation.

By the age of thirty-four, I found myself at the end of another marriage. I was also raising two beautiful children on my own. There were so many red flags in the beginning, but I chose to ignore my worth and choose companionship over truth. In the beginning of the relationship, I dealt with continual infidelity. I kept failing at relationships when all I ever wanted was to be in a healthy relationship where the love is reciprocated. Two years after my divorce, I found myself in a "situationship" with a man from work. A situationship is a mirage of a true, authentic relationship. Many times, it has toxic outcomes.

This relationship led me down a path of toxicity for four years. During the first year, things were normal—only to come to the end of that year and find out that I was *one of eight* different women. He was high-tempered, so he yelled and talked negatively. I was struggling financially because I contributed money to every delusional situation he presented to me. If we had a disagreement, he ghosted me for several weeks. When my mother passed away, he wasn't there to offer any support or comfort.

It wasn't until I found myself homeless for four months, and I lost everything after using my finances to support his fictitious dreams, did I realize the damage I was doing to myself. I realized that I was dealing with these things because I didn't know myself. The divorce left me feeling empty, rejected, lonely and insufficient. Over the last four years, I made the decision to unapologetically wear my crown consistently. As I look back, I realize that I spent twenty-five years searching to find myself. Finally, I found her!

I have been purging the past, forgiving myself, and forgiving those individuals who have hurt me. I never gave myself the opportunity to heal. Instead, I bounced from one relationship in expectation of time healing my wounds. I don't agree with the old wise statement, "Time heals all wounds." Actually, the process of forgiveness heals wounds. I had to spend time alone to learn and appreciate myself.

I never took the time to learn myself. I knew I didn't want to be alone. I didn't realize that, after multiple years of traumatic experiences and relationships, I had never spent time with *myself* and implemented self-care. I enjoyed taking *myself* out on dates. I realized that loneliness and being alone are two different things. Society has a way of making women feel like they are not enough because they are single.

What I never realized before is that I hold the power to let go of the hurt and turn toward the positive. You must speak healthy thoughts over your life and believe in yourself. Speak life into yourself with affirmation, which will lead to positive manifestations. Through the years, people always asked me how to say my name and what the meaning of my name is. I always answered with secret irritation. I felt like a broken record. I would reply, "My name is pronounced Shavaughn, but spelled Siobhan. It is Irish. It means "royalty."

Over the years, I repeated the meaning of my name. It was not until four years ago that I realized what I was calling myself. The whole time my name meant royalty! Wow! Queens wear crowns. The entire time, I was royalty and never realized it. Although I wear the crown consistently, I must maintain the position of self-worth. Wearing your crown consistently, and being unapologetic about it, is a constant fight.

It's a constant fight to keep your peace and not settle. Wearing your crown consistently is a choice and a lifestyle. It is a way of life. Surround yourself with like-minded people who will pour love into you. Pray and meditate. Embrace where you are and live each day like it is your last. Do not wait to live until you get a spouse. If you are single, live anyway. Don't settle! Be the best you that you can be. You owe it to yourself!

RECROWNING & Reflection

1. What does self-worth mean to you?

   _____

   _____

   _____

   _____

   _____

2. How has your perception of the queen you are changed over time?

   _____

   _____

   _____

   _____

   _____

3. How do you maintain your crown in the face of temptation to take it off?

ABOUT THE AUTHOR

Siobhan R. Flynn

To read her writings is to read transparency. Author Siobhan Renee' has a passion for helping women recognize their potential and overcome barriers to healthier mindsets, self-love and relationships. Siobhan's passion is to embrace women who have been broken by toxic experiences to rebuild their lives through sharing her experiences of toxicity. She has experienced firsthand what it feels like to be mistreated, verbally abused, and what it's like to rise from the debris of negativity. Siobhan has helped many men and women onto their path of healing mind, body and spirit. She can embrace an individual right where they are, without judgment, and show compassion. As a medical professional, she has seen people at their worst and she is wired to assist those with the debris left from life's situations.

Siobhan is known as the "Queen of All Trades" because she wears multiple hats in her purpose. After ten years of motivational sessions with her students, Siobhan decided to create a door that would lead to another platform of encouragement through her writing. Past experiences inspired her to write and self-publish her first book *"Journal Pages of a Virtuous Woman: Role of a Wife"* in 2016. She has also had several radio interviews on healthy relationships and self-awareness. In 2019, she wrote and directed her first stage play, "The Beauty Shop Chronicles," which focused on women empowerment. In 2020, Siobhan's efforts led her to write and self-publish her second book, *"This New Normal: A 21-Day Devotional for Frontliners."* This was a project inspired by the pandemic and being a participant of the 48-hour challenge, "How to write a 30-day devotional in 48 hours" with Tenita C Johnson.

For more information, call 313.629.5045 or email Journalpages@outlook.com. You can also stay connected with Siobhan on Instagram at @Siobhan_renee, on Facebook at Facebook.com/journalpages, or on YouTube at Siobhan Renee'.

The Art of Forgiveness

Keila D. Brintley

> *"To forgive is to set a prisoner free and discover that the prisoner was you."*
> –LEWIS B. SMEDES

What happens when you cannot forgive? Moreso, what happens when you cannot forgive yourself? We torture ourselves and we end up in self-sabotage. The guilt begins to eat you alive. Unforgiveness can be the very thing that keeps you from moving forward. It will make you sick and cause you to lose sleep. It's been known to cause anxiety, depression and stress. It sets the tones of your relationships within yourself, family, friends and even coworkers. We must be aligned with ourselves before we can be aligned with anyone else.

When I first learned about the art of forgiveness, I thought it was something fancy someone made up. It truly is an *art*. We know that art is simply defined as a skill in conducting any human activity, sincerity and knowledge. It's a skill. Skills are learned. You have to *learn* to forgive you. For you to forgive, you must accept an apology. You must let something go, purge that thing, or wipe the slate completely clean. The Word is clear: God places all of our sins in the sea of forgetfulness.

One time, my crown heavily tilted, but it did not fall off.

On April 6, 2018, I sent a text message that forever changed my life. I heard a voice on the inside of me telling me not to send it, but I decided to be petty. I had been in a six-year relationship that had ended. I had moved on with someone new, or so I thought. My ex-fiancé periodically called to check on me and, every chance I got, I served him the business. He did not keep his promises. He told me he would marry me. We had the best friendship that I've ever shared with any guy. Anyone who knew us knew how much he loved me. I *knew* he did.

I laughed with him all the time. Laughter is the best medicine, and he gave me doses of that daily. We could look at something or someone, and look at one another, and we knew exactly what the other was thinking. He was my confidant, my comforter and my companion. He spoiled me. He treated me like a queen, and he treated me like the world revolved around me, and only me. I loved him for it. I had never experienced a man treating me with such great esteem. He had my pedestal held high and not one time did I imagine falling off.

Proverbs 16:24 (KJV) says, *Pleasant words are as a honeycomb, sweet to the soul, and health to the bones.*

In 2016, he fell gravely ill. I did not know this would change our plans in life forever. I thought it was just a pitstop. I thought things would turn around. He always appeared to be in high spirits. I tried to keep life as normal as possible. So, did he. He still tried to date me, even though it took everything in him to make it out those days. By this time, he was on a walker. I struggled because he was such a strong man in his work ethic, and he had a strong personality. To see him decline in his health was heartbreaking and devastating.

I cringe at the thought of some of the things I said, as if I did not want to accept how sick he really was at the time. He promised to marry me. I would respond with, "Let's just go and do it!"

He said, "Not right now and not like this."

What I didn't know was that he was getting sicker daily. He hid some of the things the doctor said from me. I constantly sent him healing Scriptures and healing songs of motivation. He loved those. I wanted him to know and believe that God could turn things around. In this relationship, I was stronger spiritually—outwardly, anyway. He believed in God. He just didn't do the church thing, and I was good with that. He never came between me and my God, so I respected the respect that he had for me and my faith.

The day I sent the text, I was in my own feelings. I was at work, thinking, *How can you just waste someone's time and think you can get away with it?* The more I thought about it, the angrier I became. I could feel my heart palpitating. My stress levels were rising. I had literally worked myself up with ill thoughts. I totally dismissed the fact that he was ill. I thought about all the times I helped him through his illness. He was such a private person, so I became the gatekeeper of his illness with our mutual friends and kept them at bay. I managed some of his personal business and finances. That should have counted for something.

I was loyal and, to a fault, in a debilitating way. I gave my heart and soul to this man. It was time for him to cash in on his promises. At this point, I deserved it, whether he was sick or not. That was such a childish and selfish thought. But, when you have a discontent soul, you feel like the world should stop for you. I pulled out my tally book and checked the list of all the things I'd done. It was time to pay the piper. One thing I have learned is that you cannot make a person do anything they don't want to do. Discontentment will have you trying to quench a thirst you will never fulfill. It will also cause you to feel entitled. You must put that spirit in check. I learned the hard way that things are seldom what they seem to be.

"He proposed to me!"

He immediately responded by text with, "What did you say?"

"I said, 'Yes!'"

I didn't receive a response. My heart caved because I sent that text with such maliciousness. I decided to delete it immediately after I sent it because I didn't want to remind myself of how malicious I was being. I expected him to pick up the phone and call. I was going to tell him I was lying. But there was a part of me that still needed validation. That Thursday, he didn't call. I called him Friday, and he did not answer. This man has never gone without answering my calls. I thought, *I really did it this time. He is tired of my childish games.*

By this time, I was concerned. That Saturday, I had some trees removed from my yard. Some were dying and some had died already. They were starting to drop heavy branches into the yard when the lightest wind blew. I did not want them to cause any severe damage. Having them removed was the best solution. These trees became symbolic for me though. I absolutely love trees. I study them in my own time. It's one of my weird hobbies. I did everything in my own power to save two of them. I used Google to create concoctions in my attempt to save them. One remedy seemed as if it was working. There was hope for a while. I took several pictures as the tree cutters cut them down. I was going to forward the pictures to my ex-fiancé to break the ice. That was the least I could do. I knew I had to repair the relationship and clear up the lie I told. I had to fix this. I didn't know how powerful my words were at the time.

Proverbs 18:4 says, *The words of a man's mouth are as deep as waters, and the well spring of wisdom as a flowing brook.*

On Sunday, April 8, 2018, I received a call from a mutual good friend of ours. She said, "I wanted to call and tell you that I just received a call. Your friend died."

I just sat there for a moment. I could not process what she was saying. My body went numb. My best friend had left this earth and the last thing I'd said to him was a *lie*. She tried her best to make me feel better. My best friend had left this earth, thinking I had moved on. In reality, I truly hadn't. *Did he take his last breath because of what I said? Did I change the course of his life by lying? Did my words hurt him, and he gave up on living?*

I immediately called his mom. I knew my friend would not lie, but I needed to hear it from his mom. She answered and she confirmed it. She could barely talk, and neither could I. We just cried. This could have been what was going to happen eventually, but the guilt of our last conversation wanted me to believe that I sped up the process. I may never get that answer. But one thing I do know is that he knew how much I loved him. It's not the way I thought our friendship would end. I am thankful for the good times and the encouraging words I sent while he was living. I later learned that he hid more things from me because he knew I would be upset. I believe he truly did want me to move on and be happy with someone else. He knew how ill he was. He knew he could not keep his promises—not because he didn't want to—he simply could not. God had other plans.

You never know when it will be the last time you see someone. Always treat them like it will be your last time. The trees being removed from the front of my house the day before his death were parallels for me. Trees are strong. They give shade in the summer, and they give wood in the winter. They provide oxygen and they shield you from many storms. That's what he was for me. He was everything those trees represented.

My favorite movie is *The Wizard of* Oz. There are so many references throughout this movie that can lead you to freedom. My favorite reference is the Wicked Witch of the East or West. What do they have to do with forgiveness? They have absolutely nothing to do with it. However, it will show you that the enemy has no power in your life. Think about the movie. The wicked witch harassed Dorothy the whole time. The wicked witch represents unforgiveness, guilt, shame and misery. There are times when you will feel like you just don't want to go on.

Your mind is the most powerful tool you have. Most of us have heard the saying, "If you believe you are or if you believe you aren't, either way, you are right." Ephesians 4:23 says, ...*and be renewed in the spirit of your mind*. Your mind can be a battlefield. When you have negative thought after negative thought, what happens? You began to believe what you are thinking. You began to even speak aloud what you are thinking. *What you say flows from what is in your heart*, according to Luke 6:45.

Some people do not notice that they carry pain so deep inside that, when they talk to other people, they make them want to scatter. You are not those negative thoughts. It can be extremely difficult to forgive others, and it can be that much harder to forgive ourselves. It's a heavy burden to carry. No matter what your situation is, you must forgive yourself if you truly desire to live in peace.

When the Good Witch came to give Dorothy the red glittery shoes, she told her to put them on and never take them off. They must be powerful, or the wicked witch wouldn't want them so badly. She gave her a list of specifics. She said, "You must get the broom from the enemy, the wicked witch. Take her power back. After you do that, you must see a man that will have the tools to get you to the location you need to be in. Click your heels three times and believe, and you be free." Well, for Dorothy, it was home. For me, it was freedom to forgive myself. God will never leave you without instructions on how to live the best life He designed for you. The enemy wants to steal your joy, just as the witch wanted those shoes. Hold tightly onto your faith. It's going to free you.

"Life goes on" sounds so harsh when you are in the middle of a battle. The reality is *it does*. Life does not stop. We waste countless days giving away our energy to things that we should not allow to control us. First Corinthians 14:33 tells us, God is not the author of confusion, but of peace. I know it's easier said than done. There are some things you will have to fight for. The feelings I had from the lie I told to my friend did not disappear because I decided I was going to forgive myself. I had to *fight* for it.

Remember the new guy? He helped pull me up from a bottomless pit. He committed to being my true friend. Most importantly, he committed to being there after my other friend died. God will send you people to be there for you when you need. He is a comforter. God saw this day happening way before I did. So many days, I felt so alone. We can mentally alienate ourselves when we struggle with unforgiveness. I remember telling my new friend that I felt so alone.

He said, "You got me and God. That is all you need. You are going to make it through this because you aren't going down on my watch." Some people asked me how he was able to watch me grieve over someone else. He was able to do that because he had a heart full of compassion. First Peter 4:8 says, *Above all, love each other deeply, because love covers a multitude of sins*. It is imperative to have people who breathe life into you when you are down. Your circle determines if you will make it out of your dark days. Look around you to see who you allow to speak over you daily. Your tribe is your vibe. If you want to heal from unforgiveness, you must know your tribe. If they aren't pouring good things into you, it's time to find another tribe.

I want to live, not die. I was slowly dying on the inside. My new friend sent me motivational speeches, Scriptures and jokes. He also knew I loved listening to Steven Furtick of Elevation Church. He sent me morning devotional messages from him, as well. That daily dose of positive speaking is what kept me going. It was the oasis I needed in the middle of my desert of unforgiveness. During this time of trying to climb out of the bottomless pit, I gained an excessive amount of weight. My hair started falling out and I didn't want to live. For countless days, I came home from work and went straight to bed. I slept until it was time for work again. The guilt consumed me.

I do not think anyone knew the real struggle outside of my friend and my daughter. I was a high-functioning depressed person. It is not good to have these emotions eat you up inside. They can fester into many illnesses. What's on the inside must come out. You get to choose what you will birth and purge from your body. You can either live with those dead emotions or purge them. Being free requires you to take self-inventory. Solitude is not always a bad thing when you're healing. It's good to take time to reflect on what you need to change. More importantly, be true to you.

Unforgiveness can be a part of the grieving process. No one can tell you how long you should grieve. If you must get help, do just that. Talk to a trusted friend or family member. See your doctor or find a therapist. Release these things. I always wondered if my new friend would get tired of me rehashing the same conversation. I decided to ask him one day and he said, "No. I'm not tired of listening to you." I would imagine that any good friend would tell you that. I'm grateful for his listening ears. I'm sure some days, I sounded like Charlie Brown's grandmother to him.

The enemy loves to make you feel like you must deal with things alone. He wants you to waddle in your self-pity and misery. He has one job—maybe three—depending on who is telling it. His job is to steal, kill and destroy. We are not going to just hand him our hearts and minds. We have bigger missions to accomplish. There is no need to block our blessings. Many times, we are standing in our own way. Cry, if you must. Scream, if you must. But let it out. Do not allow this thing to control you any longer.

I had to shift my crown and place it back on the top of my head. I had to make peace with the fact that I just could not change what I had done and said to my old friend. I could no longer hold a grudge against myself. I'm worth forgiving. I deserve it from myself for myself. I couldn't get anything done in the earth while I was walking around downtrodden. I prayed to God, "I know he is there with you. Can you let him know that I am sorry that I lied? He needs to know the truth." I had heard all my life that anything is possible with God. So, I'm inclined to believe the message was delivered. It was the true beginning of my healing process.

God sent my new friend to me to help me transition. I realized I still had work to do. I didn't realize how many blessings I was blocking and how many connections I'd passed up when I was operating in unforgiveness. Whatever God has for me, I want it all. I gave into the calling and purpose God placed on my life. I ran for a long time. One way the enemy tries to trap you is by telling you that you are not qualified. You *are* qualified. I do not care what you have done. Forgive yourself and be free. Authentic love of oneself is the best gift you can give yourself. Nothing can penetrate through self-love. If it does, you are quickly reminded that something foreign is breaching security. In this case, security would be your mind and heart. Be sure to guard your heart and mind.

The body rejects what is foreign. It will find its way out through sickness or just by you simply releasing it. Release it. Find things to laugh at daily. Find them on purpose. Make a conscious effort to forget unpleasant events quickly. I want you to say to yourself, "I forgive myself for _____ _____."

Close your eyes and imagine yourself putting whatever it is you want to release in your hands. When you make that confession, open your hands and release it. Genuine forgiveness will free you. I want you to accept that God has already forgiven you. He does not remember a thing. You will have to work on this daily. This is not a one-stop shop. Do the work every single day. You will notice yourself getting stronger and your faith being restored. Forgiveness must be intentional. Never think you are weak because you decided to forgive. You are stronger because you decided you did not want to be caged by unforgiveness and guilt any longer.

Forgiveness is a skill. It's an art. Let's *master* the art. Listen, let's not allow this thing called unforgiveness to control you any longer. There is deliverance in forgiveness. There is absolutely no reason to camp out there. Let's shake off the guilt, unacceptance and bondage. Honey, it's time to get free from that thing. From this day forward, you will make a conscious decision to move in the direction of forgiving you! It is God's will.

Proverbs 15:4 (KJV) says, *A wholesome tongue is a tree of life: but perseverance therein is a breach of the spirit.*

RECROWNING & Reflection

1. What does forgiveness look like for you?

   _____

   _____

   _____

   _____

   _____

2. What steps will you take for your own personal growth to move toward forgiveness?

   _____

   _____

   _____

   _____

   _____

3. What does peace look like for you?

4. What can you do to shut down the negative voices in your head?

5. What does your tribe look like? Do you need a new tribe to speak life into you? Do you have a trusted friend to help hold you accountable for getting free?

ABOUT THE AUTHOR

Keila D. Brintley

When you redesign your mindset, you realize your most valuable things are stored in your heart, not a safe. Author and podcast host, Keila D. Brintley exemplifies this as she strives to live a life of wholeness. With deliberate devotion and persistent planning, she has thrived through the battlefield of her mind while positively influencing others to be free from the weight of guilt, shame and unforgiveness. After ascending above the devastation of divorce and the death of a dear friend, she also crushed imposter's syndrome. Through the process, she learned her father was right when he advised her that the easiest way to retaliate is to simply live well.

Keila is known by her social media followers as "Little Oprah" because of her penchant for initiating engaging conversations. Answering the call to create her own platform led her to start the All the Way There podcast. In a candid, yet compassionate tone, Keila and her co-host,

Tonya Dixson, facilitate thought-provoking discussions. Since 2020, the show has built a tangible connection with its audience through transparent and insightful commentary on sage topics such as mental health.

As a domestic violence survivor and advocate, she has publicly spoken about her experiences on numerous platforms. Through her words and deeds, she supports others during their struggles, encouraging them to embrace the joys of life. The devoted mother notes her daughter, Angel, as her "ray of light in my dark times. She is my motivation to win. When I look back, I'm in awe of how far I've come. My failures only showed me that there had to be another way to get something done. It has also allowed me to evolve and see the world without judgment."

Keila shares her storied journey in *Recrowning God's Daughters*, an anthology featuring stories of healing and restoration after failure. The multifaceted influencer reveals how she is mastering the art of forgiveness and reclaiming her crown by embracing her vulnerability, acknowledging her emotions, practicing her faith and seeking therapy.

Connect with Keila via email at Allthewaytherepodcast@gmail.com. Access and follow All the Way There podcast on Facebook, Twitter, Instagram, YouTube, Spotify, iTunes and Google podcasts.

The Crooked Crown

Claira Smith

What if I told you my crown was crooked because of the church? The church saw and prophesied greatness but did not challenge my comfort zone. The church pushed a gift that was needed in the ministry yet neglected me as a person. We all have purpose. We all have crowns. But your circle, or lack thereof, greatly influences if you ever understand the greatness of your crown.

I knew I had a crown at an early age. I stood before the church and proclaimed Jesus as my Lord and Savior at eleven years old. I knew I had a purpose and that it was a *great* one. I knew I had promises because I was Abraham's heir. I knew my identity wasn't rooted in material things. I understood that the Bible called me blessed, fearfully and wonderfully made, peculiar and prosperous. I've always known I had a crown, and I had a basic understanding of what it was.

Yet, my crown was never straight. It never sat tall like the crowns of other women I idolized.

Mine was *crooked*.

My grandmother's favorite verse was Proverbs 6:6: "*Go to the ant, thou sluggard; consider her ways, and be wise.*" This was the subtle way to let us know we were lazy, and we needed to get up and do something. Otherwise, we were out of the will of God. Of course, my grandmother never said that explicitly; however, we understood what was being implied. There wasn't much room for debate about it either. We could attempt to argue our humanity, but eventually, everyone would comply.

My grandmother was a devout Christian; she was just new to the job. I had the privilege of growing up with new or, often referred to as, "baby" Christians. Naturally, as a body of believers, we will always be ecstatic that someone gave their life to Christ. However, unless they have leadership that is genuinely invested, and until they have a better understanding of who God is and how He operates, they are extremely passionate, but they lack the wisdom/knowledge in order to operate properly. Because of their passion, they expect the same level of excitement and work ethic from everyone connected to them. They are on a mission to save the world and their family is first on their list. What they learn, the family has to learn. New Christians expect their family to operate like they operate.

My grandmother was the new Christian, and her children and grandchildren were her first mission. If I had one word to summarize her character, it would be *servant*. Serving in the church and serving her "neighbor" is what I remember her most for. Serving is what she taught us. From Sunday morning service and Bible study on Wednesday, to prayer meetings on Saturday, if the church had any extracurricular activities planned, the Smith household was in attendance. Because we were never there to just spectate and fill a seat, we had to be early. We were stagehands, actors and the audience. I still hear her voice yelling, "You've got to serve!" Because of that teaching, I have been in every department at the church. I've been an usher, nurse, Jr. deacon, altar worker, janitor, administrator, assistant to the administrator, and even teacher. I also served on the hospitality committee. If there was an empty spot at the church, we were taught to fill the position before we were asked and without complaint. Of course, learning to serve your neighbor, family and church is not a bad thing. It is part of our purpose as believers.

However, it became a great hiding place for me, which is where my crown began to shift.

Coming home from school one day, I was greeted at the door by my uncle.

"Have you seen the broom?" he asked.

I had been gone all day, so my answer was simple.

"No," I said as I went upstairs to my room. From that simple question, the situation escalated. He called me out of my name and spoke many hurtful derogatory things. Left in the room for hours, listening to him spew the most hurtful words I'd ever heard, I wondered what I'd actually did wrong. I got a hold of my cousin and, thankfully, she picked me up and took me to my mother. Walking in the church and seeing my mother, I finally felt safe enough to break down. They held me while I cried. The pastor saw me and had a few details of what happened. He called me up and had me assist with the altar call. I prayed and prophesied while other ministers tried to make me laugh in between. I helped clean up after service was over. However, after service ended and my family and I went home, there was no further discussion of what happened with my uncle.

Serving is a beautiful thing. Proverbs 19:17 promises a great reward when you help the poor. Matthew 5:16 details how being seen working benefits not only the one you're helping, but those who see and how it glorifies God. But the disconnect for me was the heart behind it. I was found feeding those without homes and offered my time and talent to the church. However, they did not pay attention to the fact that I had hurt and insecurities. I was struggling with a lack of identity. It's an easy façade to uphold. But I had the look of humility and holiness, but it was never my truth.

Instead of the biblical truth of who I am, my upbringing shaped my identity, purpose and worth. My worth was determined by what I could *do*. My purpose was rooted in neglecting self in order to serve. That's what it looked like to love God. As long as I served, the hurt I was experiencing would eventually go away. If I wasn't serving someone else or serving in the church, I wasn't doing my due diligence. The longer I walked in agreement with the lie, the more my crown shifted.

I gave my life to Christ as a child. So, essentially, yes, I had a little more of an understanding of what my crown was. But my foundation wasn't solid. I was growing in religion and rhetoric, not relationship. I learned how to look the part, but I never learned to actually *live and be* the part.

I had the crown. I just never knew how to wear it.

Because I was the oldest, I was a Christian, and I was a leader, I felt I wasn't the priority. My gifts and time were priority. I was expected to serve. My needs and wants were somewhere down the line. Hiding the parts of me I felt weren't appropriate for a Christian girl, I pushed the "good Christian" narrative, causing my crown to shift even more.

Afraid of disappointing God, my family and the church, I was buried beneath titles and hats I was forced to wear. I was forced to be the example, which left little room for life experience. Growth, maturity and discovering who you are comes from living and making mistakes. However, I became so afraid of making a mistake that I didn't live. I confined myself to church, work and school. I didn't make a decision without figuring out how that decision could or would affect my family. I made myself constantly available to my family and the church, financially, emotionally, mentally and physically. If I had it, and they needed it, I would sacrifice it.

This became my motto with everyone I came into relationship with. I stood behind them as their cheerleader, assistant, encouragement and coach when necessary. I grew up burned out, not understanding why the passion I once had for God and His people was dwindling down to nothing. Anger and resentment toward myself and God grew in me. I gave up "normalcy" and myself for my relationship with God. I was convinced that the sacrifices I made were in vain. If the greatness others saw in me was actually there, why didn't I see it or believe it? Why did fear of failure and disappointing others hold me hostage for so long?

Adjusting my crown to its rightful position meant unlearning who I *thought* I was and what it meant to be Christian. We are queens in God's kingdom. It is our kingdom right to be prosperous. Religion has taught many generations that lack is the key to pleasing God. Ignoring yourself and giving your all to your neighbor and the church is considered holiness. I still very much believe in serving in the church and serving my fellow man, but within context. I laid my crown down to help everyone else stay afloat in an effort not damage my crown. However, I came second to everyone and everything else. Taking time for myself, and investing in the things I wanted to do, almost felt like sin. Being so readily available to others made my purpose very dispensable.

It didn't matter what God told me to do. Fear of not being good enough for the call, and feeling the need to be there for others, my work always ended up on the back burner. Constantly serving was a great cover up for deeper issues and insecurities. My theology was severely flawed. I didn't have to deal with my worth being rooted in being needed. My worth as a Christian, a woman, sister and friend was determined by what I could do for others. I never had to deal with the thoughts of not being good enough for God's call because I was helping my leaders and/or my family. If I was serving someone else, that was good enough for my Christian walk. It shouldn't have mattered that it didn't match exactly what God told me to do. Right?

I wasn't completely healed. My crown looked better safely stored away anyway. I entertained the thought that maybe it would even look good on someone else. The leaders of the church were full of people who lived to tell the tale. My story was boring, to say the least. My story didn't match the beauty of my crown. The misconception that tragedy was the prerequisite for purpose kept my crown safely locked away.

Not understanding the importance of boundaries, the beauty that is my testimony, and the biblical truth of who God says I am, is what caused me to take off my crown. My crown was never important enough to me, let alone anyone else. My family did what they could with what they had. They gave me a good foundation on what it meant to serve God. Truth be told, we were learning together; they just had the upper hand with age. What they knew to be the truth, unfortunately, had to be my truth for the time being. I was convinced that making other people more of a priority than myself was me being a good Christian. I thought as long as I was sacrificing, I was making God proud. I kept myself in a constant place of lack in multiple areas of life because I thought that is what would make me a good person.

If I wore my crown, I wouldn't be humble. If I said, "No," I wasn't doing right by my neighbor. My adult years were spent downplaying who I was as a person, as a queen. My crown never sat properly on my head. As I mentioned earlier, I've always had my crown, but wearing it correctly was my issue. It was always *crooked*.

Realizing my crown was crooked happened when I finally sat down and did nothing. The Lord sat me down. I was no longer active in ministry. Family couldn't depend on me like they were once able to. I moved to Chicago temporarily and was basically by myself. In those moments, the Lord could actually deal with me. He showed me the many areas I had avoided for far too long. He showed me how it was okay to ask for help or just be fed spiritually, without having to serve.

One night, I was lying in bed and God spoke, "Crooked tiaras."

He showed me how a lack of understanding of purpose, identity and worth had kept me from tapping into my true potential. One day, I would be able to show others how to straighten their tiara. He showed me how He loved me just because of who He is. Overall, the Lord graced me with a break to reflect and regroup.

Straightening my crown started when I changed my church. I came home from Chicago, and I told my pastor that God told me that I wasn't growing because I was too close with my family. My godfather was the pastor and 80% of the church was my family. They saw that I was active in ministry, serving in the church, and had a decent relationship with God. So, that was good enough for them.

My comfort zone was comfortable for everybody else. He agreed that it was time for me to go and he gave me his blessing. I wandered for a while, but I found a church that could push me to Christ. I instantly fell into old patterns of "serving," but it didn't last long. I was pushed. We not only talked about what I could do to aid in the growth of the church, but also what the church could do to ensure Claira was growing. The callings of God on my life were right at the forefront. Leadership pushed for the whole person, not just for the parts of me that could help grow the ministry.

When they saw I was burned out, they encouraged me taking time for myself and actually going on vacations. The vision I had of myself changed when my circles changed. My friendships were genuine. I encountered women who were just happy to know and be around me. They weren't looking for me financially, as a minister or as a counselor. The friendships I formed over the last three years were ones that taught me it was okay to embrace and love me.

In the areas where my crown was once crooked, or completely off, they have adjusted and prayed me back into position. I allowed myself to dream and started to take a chance on myself. The covenant connections God has allowed me to make were ones who see my potential. However, they have no intentions on monopolizing or monetizing off of it. They help me see the gifts and potential within myself and encourage me to go for it 120%.

For me, the crown represented purpose and identity. My purpose wasn't as important as the next. How I saw myself didn't fit the mold of what God was calling me to do. Wearing it didn't seem befitting. So, I accepted the thought that maybe my crown was simply best worn behind the scenes while helping others with their crown. In a sense, that is part of my purpose. But because of a broken foundation, my purpose was perverted. The only way I can show my sisters how to wear their crown is to proudly wear mine. That means walking boldly in my purpose, no longer pushing myself to the background, nor suppressing who I am or what I want in life for the sake of others. Every day, I have to choose to take responsibility for myself and live the life God has called me to live. My crown is necessary—not only to the kingdom—but for me. Yes, I have gifts, callings and a great purpose. But sometimes, wearing my crown simply requires me simply just be.

I still very much agree with serving, just not when it's become your identity, or it becomes your basis for holiness and sanctification.

As God is repositioning my crown into its proper place, I am learning more what it looks to like to be Christian. I am learning that wearing my crown means to be confident in who Christ has called me to be, unapologetically. Wearing your crown is accepting your individuality. We are one body with many different parts and functions. No two Christians are the same. No one has the same purpose. We have to learn our part and function in the body of Christ as our authentic selves. Knowing that God called me and knowing what He called me to do, is vital to me wearing my crown properly. He reaffirmed my worth. It wasn't rooted in what I did and how well I did it. My worth was established at the thought of my creation. I don't have to prove it.

Your worth never changes; just your understanding of it. Once you realize that you are worth more than rubies, your walk changes and how you present yourself changes. You no longer beg for attention. You don't beg for people to see you.

My crown is yet shifting into its proper place. I'm learning to give myself grace through the process and love myself along the way.

RECROWNING & Reflection

1. If you grew up in church, what are you doing to take care of the whole person?

2. How is your circle (church friendships family) aiding in your overall growth?

3. How have you used serving as a cover-up in the past?

ABOUT THE AUTHOR

Claira Smith

$\mathcal{P}$rophetess Claira Smith has grown in grace by challenging the very foundation that she grew up on. Operating in ministry for almost ten years, it wasn't until recently that she was able to find her lane. Taking the step and officially accepting the call to ministry in August of 2018, Claira was affirmed a prophet. Teaching biblical truth and helping women understand who God says they are, instead of the narrative life forced on them, has become a passion for Claira. Because of that passion, she launched the ministry of Crooked Tiaras. The goal is to deal with biblical teachings of purpose, worth and identity in order to teach the next generation to wear their crowns correctly.

She has had the privilege of speaking at numerous women's conferences, discussing topics such as being fearlessly restored, the woman behind the mask, and countless others. In 2021, Claira accepted the *Dare to be Fearless Woman of the Year Award*. Claira has dared to step out on faith and proudly share her story in the anthology, *Recrowning God's Daughters* where she details the false teaching that caused her to wear her crown crooked and how God ultimately straightened it.

Connect with Claira via email at crookedtiaras2016@gmail.com. Keep up with her ministry, Crooked Tiaras, on Instagram @_crookedtiara.

The Bent & Broken Crown

Deanna M. Ferguson

"Mama, are you gonna get off the couch?" the little one asked.

"No!" my inner voice shouted. "I'm going to lay here until everything changes." All I could feel was rage! My body lay limp, exhausted from trying to prevent my inner demise. My brain was convulsing. Hezekiah Walker's *Power Belongs to God* was playing on the house speaker, fighting to envelope my rage. But that rage was pouring into the atmosphere like scaling hot tea from a screaming kettle relieved of her pressure.

I was livid with every man I had ever known. My father for rejecting my attempts to act as a first-born son. My brother for being born years later but getting to have his own room while I had to share with my sisters or be put in the den. My godbrother for being favored more by my mother than me. The wrong thinking tied to memories and offenses merged in and out of years. I was angry at my boss, pastor, father, brother, son and husband for lessening my value as a human being, let alone as a woman, because I had views that were different from theirs. To be a girl or woman passionate about anything of substance, or show any kind of emotion, was distasteful and unattractive not only to men, but everyone! Today, women still tell their daughters, nieces, cousins, co-workers and friends that no one wants to listen to the "angry Black woman." (Beloved, there is nothing wrong with being angry, Black or woman—or any combination thereof!)

If Mephibosheth (2 Samuel 4:4) was physically damaged from being dropped, I don't know how I was able to function at all because my soul was surely shattered. Every tear that fell reminded me of broken glass piercing my heart, mind and intellect. It's funny when I look back on that time, I realize now that God wanted me to heal. But first, I had to acknowledge that I was sick. I was overwhelmed by bitterness and unforgiveness for people I thought were supposed to love and protect me. I wanted them to be loyal to me like I felt an obligation of loyalty to them. I didn't realize at the time, but I wasn't sure what loyalty meant. Later, I came to understand that I wasn't practicing true loyalty, but *idolatry*. I wanted to be accepted so badly by people I thought I couldn't do or live without.

Drifting, I could feel myself being transported back to the house on the westside, where I grew up and where I first remembered the things that happened to me earlier in life. It was an unshakable, reoccurring dream that often sucked me in, then drowned me in fear, hurt, anger and sometimes hatred. It's where my tiny crown was pulled off and thrust into a corner, while I was painfully molested. Then, I had word curses so powerfully spoken over me that it would erase my memory. If I remembered, it might literally suck the life out of my tiny body. I listened to the radio and Gospel music to soothe my soul. It even created a joy and boldness in me that sent me to that dreadful corner, where I would mentally try to pry my bent and broken crown out of dusty drywall full of wooden splinters and rusty nails. I sang songs of Zion and lifted my hands like I had seen the old church mothers do while they silently shed tears to the God of their salvation. I wonder now if those tears were full of the same kinds of burdens that caused my spirit to stoop and bend under the fear of rejection and devaluation.

A byproduct of losing one's crown can be hatred. I am not sure when it surfaced, but at some point, I hated a lot of people. Hoping to lessen the pain of them rejecting or hating me, I was miserable as a child. Busy in the very beginning, then very guarded and intuitively stoic. Mothers, when your young girl/teenager has a "bad attitude," come closer to her. Look her in her eyes. Ask her tough, meaningful questions about her life and ask her how she feels. More times than not, she has that attitude for specific reasons. She hates all the abuse, neglect and responsibility placed on her, without knowing what to do. She hates being expected to behave as an adult or a child when it suits the adults around her. Not all our young girls are quiet and shy; some of them are brimming just beneath the surface. The only way to stay sane or out of trouble is retreating from people who are supposed to protect and support them because they are not sure who to trust.

When you are in pain, it's hard to articulate the continual dripping leviathan can leave on your wrung out soul. Nonetheless, I knew I didn't want to be in the grip of any soul- consuming enemy. I later understood that the enemy wanted to destroy my young life so that I would not have the boldness needed for the life and purpose I was given to live. In my early teens, I tried to commit suicide. I was quiet and depressed, and the only thing that quieted my spirit was going to church. The house of God was a solace and joy. However, it was also a contradiction, in terms. I attended a small Baptist church. My pastor preached fire and brimstone, and it always made me want to know and learn more. When many kids would have wanted to run and hide, my spirit sat straight up, and many times leapt within me! Instinctively, I knew God loved me and was for me, beyond any person I knew intimately.

Our foundation came from my parents holding Bible study and devotion at home. On Sundays, our pastor preached heaven down, compelling my desire and love for the Word. My pastor was loving and kind to me. That's how I remember him as a child. But he was vehemently opposed to women preaching or holding any kind of leadership position in the church. While he did not share the same doctrinal opinions of other prominent Black denominational leaders, he did share the opinion that women can "work for" men in church, but they were not to be considered senior leaders—only workers. Women could teach Sunday School to young children, but a woman's influence or ascribed value came from living virtuously. This idea that women, unlike men, could only be used by God if they were pure may not be spoken aloud, but is still very much the prevailing thought.

Today, we add educated to the list of prerequisites for women to be leaders. Women need to be titled "Doctor" or hold some form of advanced or terminal degree to be considered credible, especially in church. Men can simply say they are called to most vocations, excluding certain fields like medical doctors of course, but most fields are wide open to them. The underlying idea reveals that, based on his gender alone, a man can be a leader (especially of women), whether or not his character and ability support this assertion. It is the primary reason there is so much abuse in traditional families and churches. We do not hold those in power accountable for their actions. We allow gender to decide how they are allowed to answer. Look at all the powerful men just now being brought to accountability for the abuse of young women and girls. Many of them are of a certain age. It was more acceptable then. Everyone kept quiet or blamed the women and girls. Sadly, I am acquainted with this paradigm. We punish girls and women like we do young, helpless children if they do not comply with the rules of family or an organization. However, humanity allows men to rule, no matter their character or leadership ability.

For a woman, the other option is marriage and bearing children. An interesting directive since to create a family in its original organic state requires man and woman, not just woman. His view seemed to be that, just like women in earlier times, we only had value based on service to everyone else, except ourselves. When he talked or preached about it, he was dogmatic, unyielding and seemed to take any variation of opinion personally. Regardless of his dogmatic rhetoric, it did not change the way I loved God. Prayer and learning the Word was my solace! But at the same time, I was often confused. I wondered why God allowed people, especially His people, to devalue women and young girls so effortlessly, as if it were the sanctioned norm.

I was conflicted from the start. God called me very early to preach the Gospel. As a young girl, I told Him I did not *want* to do it, but I *would* do it … no matter what. In my mind, I was rejected from the very start.

My parents were very young when I was born. They wanted their firstborn to be a boy. While I never wanted to be a boy, I wanted to be respected as the firstborn. I have had the responsibility, joy and grace to be the "firstborn" in my family; yet, it is never the same as being the firstborn son. I think much of what I did as a young woman amounted to trying to ascribe value to myself by being as good as, or better, than the boys. While no one actually said boys are better, demonstration in mundane occurrence everywhere was evident. I was a tomboy, and I rode bicycles and big wheels with the boys. I threw rocks in the alley and fought with the boys. Partly, it was my nature. But instinctively, it was to impress my father. Before I actually liked baseball, I wanted him to take me to games and teach me about the sport so we would have something in common.

In my early twenties, I needed money for college. The tipping point to joining the Army, a male-dominated vocation, was to prove to my mother and father that I may not have been a boy, but I was worthy to be valued and respected as the firstborn. I wanted to be a singer because I thought I was pretty good, and I loved music. But my mom thought I should learn typing and shorthand. People also told me, "Good singers are a dime a dozen." But I knew God wanted me to do something creative and different. To add insult to injury, God called me to a male-dominated vocation. But in fairness to my family and loved ones, I contributed to my demise by making excuses (wrong thinking) for other people's opinions. I put their opinions before what God said about me. What do you do when you contribute to losing your crown?

I bought my first house in my thirties, under the teaching of my then pastor, whom I admired and loved dearly. By then, I was a single mom. My ex-husband did not want to buy a house with me. I initially thought it was because he didn't think we would make it as husband and wife. Truth is, I didn't think we would make it! I later learned he didn't want to buy a home in the state where we were living because he wanted to go back to his hometown. He now had a wife and children. He knew I didn't want to live near his family or mine. I wanted us to live our lives without the influence of either of our families. In my mind, it represented things I wanted to get away from. I loved my family, and he loved his. But honestly, I did not want the marriages and relationships my parents or his parents had. While I thank God for my parents, who have been married fifty-four years, I still wanted something different. I did not think I could be happy with the kind of relationship they had. Little did I know, we were both perpetuating the things we had seen in our parents and others instead of asking God to be the example for our marriage.

Excited about my accomplishment, I had a housewarming party! I invited all of my church family. They didn't need to bring anything. I just wanted them to come and celebrate this accomplishment with me. I had worked really hard. I worked three jobs, counting my reserve military duty, to provide a better quality of life for my children.

No one came that day.

My little sister and I cooked all the food and set the house up for a party. Not one person showed up. I cried like I was back in high school in the south in the AP classes with white kids who didn't think I should be there. In school, church and work, I was constantly made to feel unworthy, unwanted and unqualified. I allowed people to tell me that my life was not worth living by denying me access to the life, liberty and love others experienced.

Women, especially women of color, experience this often. I was afraid that if I didn't produce at a certain level or speed, I would be useless. In order to be accepted, I had to show everyone that I could make money, raise children, hold a job and make investments, like the Proverbs 31 woman. I love her, but I also felt if I could not live up to that ideal, my value would be diminished. I was terrified of rejection, and

I hated what it represented. Everyone wants to be loved and valued. However, I spent countless years in idolatry because I cared more about the opinions of people who didn't even like me than being in the expressed will of God.

The more material things I accumulated, the more I felt as if, at any given moment, someone would tell me I did not have the ability to be great. It was as pervasive as a silent disease that, over time, manifested irrevocable damage. I felt so isolated that God literally had to tell me through a prophet that God said stop fearing greatness! I have learned over the years that I am not the only one. Isolation is one of the companions of rejection and microaggression. When you do not fit in because God gives you a different vision and journey, instead of it being celebrated, you are ridiculed. People will tell you that you can't accomplish something you know you clearly heard God tell you that you could. It is a trick of the enemy, beloved. Stand on what you know God said, no matter how it hurts or how alone you feel. You are not the only one.

Diversity is not always celebrated by people we love; they believe unity means identical. It does not. Jesus may have looked like those who walked with Him, but He was clearly the one people sought out. It wasn't the way He dressed that made Him different; it was His life's calling. He was the healer, Savior and Son of God. He taught us how *to make disciples of all men* (Matthew 28:19). We want to be conformed to His image, not one another. It is an amazing testimony to exhibit that God is the God of various kinds of people. We are a part of the Apostle John's vision of people *no man could number* (Revelation 7:9).

An old expression says, "The devil thought he had me, but I got away!" The day I tried to take my life, I swallowed a bottle of my mother's pills. They were muscle relaxers. Immediately, I felt tingly all over. My decision seemed euphoric, romantic even. Everyone would be sorry I was gone. No one to push around and bully in school. No one to blame for things going wrong. No one to laugh at for wearing crazy clothes. But when I thought of my family, my mom and dad, rippling waves of sadness swept over me. I thought, "They won't miss me. One less kid to worry about." Warm tears slid down my cheeks onto my neck in an itching sensation. My high little mind asked, "Why does everybody hate me?"

At that moment, one of my little sisters came in as I was waiting to close my eyes for good. She crawled on the bed and hugged me. She hugged me repeatedly. She told me she loved me repeatedly. She told me she loved me and gripped me so tight that I could feel God's breath breathing on me and expressing His love through her. It felt like the day I felt when I was baptized. When my pastor dipped me, time stopped.

Under water, my heart was swelling and screaming, "Yes, Lord!" before he snatched me back up into a world of trouble.

That day, my sister squeezed me tightly. I knew that I would live, and I knew I *wanted* to live. I sat straight up, got out of bed, calmly walked in the bathroom, and jammed my hand down my throat. I did it so hard that I started jumping around like I'd hit my foot on the edge of a bed. But I wouldn't take my fingers out. I was waiting for that reflux! That reflux represented my desire to undo what I had done. Butterflies filled my stomach. I was lightheaded. However, I couldn't feel the fingers jamming my throat because adrenaline was forcing my body into subjection to my newfound will.

I was high, but sober enough to know that I almost played myself and my future generations. I have a covenant with God. I promised Him, no matter what. My future generations are already instructed to worship Him. We were born to represent Him in the earth as long as it remains! I almost came into agreement with grief, bitterness and hopelessness. But the epiphany overwhelmed me. I knew I must live. Between jumping around and holding my fingers down my throat, the rush of desperate desire to dislodge regret and fear mixed with bile filled my throat and nose.

Choking, I prayed, "Jesus, help me! You said you love me! Help me!" He did, and I am here to tell the story!

Through my little sister, God loved me enough to make me understand that no one could take His place. He would always show me. I had placed fear of rejection, unforgiveness and bitterness above His love and provision in my life, which was an unholy agreement I made with my heart and mind. God did not let me die in my ignorance and deception. He decided enough was enough. He met me right where I needed Him. One of that sister's favorite greetings is, "Jesus loves you!" Whenever I hear her say it to people, it stirs me.

I still have a hard time trying to understand some of the things God allowed into my life. I understood why people may not come to my rescue. When my mind rubs its finger over my heart, it seems like a lot of scarring. Wrong thinking had me certain that people's actions represented how God felt about me. They didn't. I had to let go of bitterness and unforgiveness. It seems like I had a different standard for myself than I had for others. I wanted to be accepted, loved and treated with respect and value. But I did not give that. No one did it for me. But God did. I was just too bitter to see it. Matthew 7:20 says, *By their fruit, you will know them.*

"I am not getting off this couch until everything changes." I missed work the next day because I couldn't lift my head. Physically, I couldn't lift my head. I was smothering from the hurt and worry I had caused myself. I went to the church with a confession of transgression. It felt like before I could get out of the meeting, everyone knew what I had done. I call it transgression because I knew what I did was wrong. It is the picture of God drawing a line in the sand and saying, "Child, this is your boundary. Do not cross it." I did not fall into wrongdoing; I knew it was wrong and I did it anyway. It was bad behavior tied to wrong thinking.

In my mind, I needed something to numb this pain and isolation I felt. If I don't say anything, no one will know. However, when you belong to God, you cannot lay down at night knowing you have been disobedient to God. You can't live contrary to your life's purpose. I had to repent! When I came to myself like the prodigal son, I went to where I thought I could receive forgiveness for repentance. That is not my testimony. Basically, I was what we call today *cancelled*. The church has been involved in that practice for quite a while. But I still went every Sunday and any other time the church doors were open. I loved God, His people, and His house. I still do.

"I am not getting off this couch until everything changes." God spoke to me and said, "You sinned against me. I told you no and you went your own way. Go to the person you hurt and tell them you are sorry. Go and apologize." So, not only did I go to the church, but I went to the person I had sinned against and apologized. I asked for forgiveness. The church didn't forgive me, but the person I hurt did. Stunned from the revelation of my confession, their eyes kinetic expression flashed like a sequence of still photos from bewilderment to anger to hurt. This swift deep cut hemorrhaging from a fresh wound was met with no questions asked, just a tight grip, breast to breast, with pure forgiveness. I walked away with blood on my soul and mind, but forgiven, nonetheless. I sat in my car, chest heaving and shortness of breath. Then, I exhaled and said, "Thank you, God, for showing me what to do."

That day, the forgiving hug I received from the person I had wronged felt like the sweetly scented hug my sister gave me all those years earlier to prevent me from ending my life. I know the circumstances were different, but I promise the same aroma of God's presence rushed in. It rushed in and changed everything!

These memories represent the years I was injured and the years I was the aggressor. Through it all, God showed me grace and mercy. He let me know that I did not have to meet a particular formula to be loved by Him. I did not have to be perfect. I don't have to measure up to someone else's standard of usefulness to be valued. He wanted my relationship with Him to be the priority. My arduous journey is filled with detailed sorrows and joys, victory and lessons, too numerous to count. Yet, my prayer is that you realize that crowning or re-crowning begins with God's love and definition of who you are. You are not what you have done or what other people have done to you. You are who God said you are. Now, walk in it!

RECROWNING & Reflection

1. What things do you need to repent for in order to regain and restore your crown?

   _____

   _____

   _____

   _____

   _____

2. Who do you need to forgive to walk in the fullness of the royalty God has called you to?

   _____

   _____

   _____

   _____

   _____

3. How have you traded material things for your crown?

_____

_____

_____

_____

_____

ABOUT THE AUTHOR

Deanna M. Ferguson

Many believe life may be hard and uncertain. This dynamic author declares, "You are strong enough to live the life you have been given!" Deanna's passion is advocating for family and community. Her life's journey has been filed with deeply held joy and profound sorrow, giving her a unique insight and empathy for hurting people. Her ministry has given her the opportunity to preach the good news of the Gospel around the United States and abroad. A licensed minister since 2007, she is known as the encourager who speaks words of affirmation and empowerment into the lives of women. Her provocative teaching encourages deeper connections, successfully navigating conflict and walking in God-given purpose.

She is an Army veteran who served over twenty-five years, receiving several military awards for achievement and service. She holds a bachelor's degree in Business from Excelsior College in Albany, New York.

Deanna is not only an author, but an artist and lifestyle influencer. Her creative and artistic credits include professional gospel recordings and performances with Steller Award Nominated Larry Callahan and Selected of God, studio recording background vocals for Dorinda Clark Cole, and various other gospel artists.

For booking and speaking engagements, email deannasherone@gmail.com or connect with her on social media @deannasherone.

ABOUT

So It Is Written

We help entrepreneurs write the ONE book that will expand their reach and get them to SIX figures in record time! Period!

As the leading content curators for six-figure authorpreneurs and entrepreneurs, So It Is Written is best known for helping them package and leverage their expertise into a bestselling book, which amplifies their brand, accelerates their paydays and attracts bigger opportunities!

Let us help you brand in excellence as an author and entrepreneur so you can develop multiple streams of income from just ONE book!

Call us at 313-777-8607 today or email info@soitiswritten.net for more details about our services. We look forward to working with you to make your project one of excellence!

CPSIA information can be obtained
at www.ICGtesting.com
Printed in the USA
JSHW041738260622
27361JS00003B/11

9 798985 020694